*The Kingdom Beyond Caste*

*Liston Pope*

no ISBN

# THE
# KINGDOM
*beyond*
# CASTE

FRIENDSHIP PRESS · NEW YORK

*Library of Congress Catalog Card Number:*
*57–6157*

MANUFACTURED IN THE UNITED STATES OF AMERICA

*To My*
*Mother and Father*
*in*
*North Carolina*

# CONTENTS

# Contents

# Contents

# Contents

Any serious discussion of the explosive question of race is likely to reveal, sooner or later, the personal credentials of those engaged in it. These credentials will have to do not only with range of experience, but also with fundamental perspectives on the nature of man and society and with the faith, or lack of it, by which one lives. However rigorously one may seek to be objective, personal attitudes and convictions color the discussion profoundly.

This book is written out of a welter of experiences involving race relations. They go back to earliest memories. The old-fashioned Negro nurse, who was a sort of second mother to the children in her care, has become rare now that opportunities for other types of work at higher salaries are more available to Negro women. But I had such a Negro nurse as a very small boy, and she possessed the splendid attributes generally ascribed to that vanished species. At least she did when I was "a good boy": stories, games, and cookies were then the order of the day. But her reaction to bad behavior was of an entirely different order. She was reported to be part-Indian, and it was said that the Indian part of her would quickly assert itself if her charges became bad children. Young imaginations could grasp the possibilities, and discipline was excellent.

From the time when my early impressions made me see people as simple stereotypes to the present moment has been a long road in terms of personal experience and of racial developments in the world. My years have been divided almost equally between growing up in the South, where race relations are of the very stuff of daily life, and adult residence in New England, with its comparatively indifferent attitudes. They have included the privilege of seeing at first hand the bewildering variety of racial patterns in Africa, and especially in the Union of South Africa; in most of the non-Communist countries of Asia; in Australia; and in the nations of Western Europe. My study and the street have been in continual competition for the time available, with the street tending to gain the advantage more recently.

## Preface

The situation in race relations has undergone profound and sweeping changes during the lifetime of the last generation, and especially during the past fifteen years. Issues of race lay rather dormant from the abolition of slavery until the rise of Nazi Germany. White dominance of most of the world was an established fact; however deep or widespread the resentment on the part of non-white peoples, explicit protests were fairly rare and generally localized.

When World War II began, approximately 750 million people, nearly all of them colored people, were still living under the colonial rule of nations predominantly white. In 1956, only about one fifth of these former subjects were still governed from abroad; most of them were in Africa, and even there the movements toward independence were gaining powerfully in many places. Within half a generation, an imperial system that had required several hundred years to build had been all but liquidated. In long perspective this may be regarded as the most significant revolution of our age. Its implications for the future are only beginning to be apparent.

Alongside the political revolution, supporting it and being supported by it, has gone a radical revision in views about racial superiority. The Japanese desired a statement about racial equality in the Versailles Treaty at the end of World War I, and were refused. Today such a statement would be regarded generally as commonplace and almost superfluous. Even in the Union of South Africa, where the debate over race is the most intense to be found in the contemporary world, the discussion has to do less with racial *superiority* than with racial *differences,* though in practical affairs the issue quickly resolves itself into one of dominance by the whites over the non-white groups.

The world-wide revolution in race relations has had its dramatic expression in the United States. Segregation of the Negro in the South, largely taken for granted for many years, is now a subject of furious controversy among policy-making groups, from the local school board to the highest political circles. No aspect of human relations, unless possibly that of relations between the United States and the Soviet Union, is of greater import in America than the race question. It has an immediacy and concreteness unmatched by problems in international affairs.

The Christian church has been deeply involved in the development of the revolution, and this book is especially concerned with that involvement. In various chapters an effort is made to elicit the implications of the Christian gospel for the idea of race and for relations between races. The connection between Christian teachings and the concept of democracy is also explored. At some points, therefore, the approach is theological or philosophical in character, as made by one who has been nurtured in the Christian faith and takes his position within it. At other points, the findings of the social sciences are drawn upon, as objectively as possible, to illumine the actual patterns and possibilities of race relations with regard to the church and within our total society. All told, this small book is an attempt to discuss one aspect of the relation of Christ to contemporary society, and to discern the lineaments of a kingdom beyond caste, already foreshadowed but yet to come.

LISTON POPE

New Haven, Connecticut
*December 1, 1956*

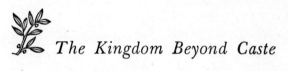 *The Kingdom Beyond Caste*

# Chapter One

## FACETS OF RACIAL STRESS

Racial feeling can express itself in an infinite variety of ways. Most often it is built into commonplace patterns of discriminatory treatment and is hardly raised into consciousness at all, though it may cause smoldering resentment on the part of those discriminated against. Sometimes it assumes a political or religious guise: the traditional preference (greatly modified in recent years) of the Negro American for "the party of Lincoln" and the centrality of the Negro church in its community are examples. More rarely, racial prejudices or frustrations explode into overt violence, exposing deep stresses that had been present all the time.

1

It is by no means to be considered that violence is characteristic in the relationship between different racial groups. But a great deal can be learned from attention to racial "incidents," provided allowance is made for the exaggerated behavior manifested in them. Symptoms generally hidden below the surface are thereby exposed. A terse summary of certain episodes of recent years will illustrate both the variety and the profundity of racial stresses in the contemporary world.

\* \* \*

Very early in 1942, soon after Pearl Harbor, the commanding general of the Western Defense Command issued an official memorandum on American policy toward persons of Japanese descent in the United States. He referred to these persons as a group (127,000 of them, of whom a large proportion were American citizens) as "potential enemies," saying that it could not be assumed "that any Japanese, barred from assimilation by convention as he is, though born and raised in the United States, will not turn against this nation when the final test of loyalty comes." He went on with the remarkable prophecy: "There are indications that these [people] are organized and ready for concerted action at a favorable opportunity. The very fact that no sabotage has taken place to date is a disturbing and confirming indication that such action will be taken."

There had actually been no instances of sabotage by

Japanese Americans at Pearl Harbor or in the tense weeks that followed the beginning of the war with Japan. Nevertheless, Japanese Americans were rounded up as a group and herded into concentration camps, often at a serious personal and economic loss. The damage to their pride in America was very obvious at the time; many renounced their American citizenship, feeling that they had been betrayed and stigmatized by their country. On the other hand, thousands of Japanese Americans were taken into the armed services and many gave outstanding service on the battlefield. Ultimately about a third were settled in the East or Middle West, where they encountered varying degrees of hostility or hospitality. At the end of the war, the remainder sought to pick up the broken threads of their lives as best they could.

The Japanese Americans were not interned simply because of their race; the excitement of war made them "the enemy." The fact remains that all members of this ethnic group were rounded up, whether or not they were suspected of political disloyalty as individuals.

\* \* \*

On the night of August 1, 1943, Harlem blew up. It was not the first riot in the Negro sections of American cities during wartime: there had been riots in Atlanta and elsewhere during and just after World War I, and there had been a serious riot in Detroit only a few weeks before the explosion in Harlem. Nor was this the first riot in Harlem: in 1935 there had been a wild uprising resulting from lack of economic opportunity during the depression and from chronic conditions of over-crowding and exploitation.

Moreover, the riot of 1943 was not strictly a "race riot," as that in Detroit had been. Whites and Negroes were not fighting one another. But racial tensions had set the stage for what became a night of looting and violence.

For weeks the population of Harlem had been agitated by stories of the mistreatment and murder of Negro soldiers in Southern camp communities, with Southern policemen as the principal offenders. It had been reported that Negro soldiers had been killed by policemen in Little Rock, Arkansas; Beaumont, Texas; Mobile, Alabama; Columbia, South Carolina; and else-where. On the night of August 1, there was an argument between a white policeman and a Negro soldier in the lobby of a hotel in Harlem. Accounts of the episode vary, but according to the most credible version, the following sequence roughly approximates the resulting events:

The quarrel ended when the policeman shot and wounded the soldier. Within a few minutes, the story that a white policeman had shot a Negro soldier in Harlem itself spread through the entire community. The streets were filled almost immediately with roaring mobs. Nearly all the plate glass windows on principal streets were smashed, and looters took over quickly. When daybreak came, six Negroes were dead, and the police estimated that 307 persons had been injured, including fifty-three policemen. Property damage was estimated at a million dollars. Only prompt and discerning action by Mayor LaGuardia, Negro leaders, and the police prevented a higher toll.

As indicated, this was not a "race riot." But the violence erupted from a matrix of racial hatred. And it illustrates the fact that racial discrimination, wherever practiced (in this case, in Southern camp communities), can have far-reaching and unintended repercussions in some other part of the world.

\* \* \*

In February, 1948, a parade of African ex-servicemen marched on Government House in the Gold Coast, ostensibly in protest against high prices, shortages of consumer goods, and other postwar hardships among the African people of that colony. More powerful in the minds and hearts of the marchers than the immediate causes of discontent was an intense nationalist sentiment that had been brewing for some decades but had boiled to the surface rapidly in the postwar years. The Gold Coast, populated almost exclusively by Africans, was resounding with a demand for self-rule and the expulsion of the British.

After more moderate methods had failed, the police opened fire on the parade and dispersed it. But comparable demonstrations rapidly became widespread in the colony, and before they were brought to an end twenty-nine persons had been killed and property damage had reached a total of two million pounds.

Today the Gold Coast is virtually a self-governing nation, though it remains under close British supervision. For the first time in any British dependency, Negroes have assumed ministerial office through popular election. The whole world, and Africa in particular, watches as a new nation begins to define its life.

\* \* \*

On January 13, 1949, at five o'clock in the afternoon, when the exit from offices and stores was at its peak, an African boy in Durban, South Africa, slapped an Indian boy in the face. Thereupon another Indian hurled the African boy against a shop window, and the latter received some minor cuts on his head. This adolescent scuffling led to riots across the city for two days. Durban, nestling quietly by the Indian Sea and in many ways comparable to Miami Beach or Biloxi, Mississippi, had been seething with racial tensions underneath its placid surface for months. Angered by petty irritations in their dealings with one another, and outraged by restrictive and oppressive policies on the part of the white government and community, Indians and

Africans now undertook to destroy one another. When the situation finally was brought under control, 142 persons had been killed, more than 1,000 had been injured, and over 2,000 buildings had been damaged or destroyed.

In protest against governmental policies of *apartheid* (literally, "apartness," though most of the policies not only enforce segregation, but also amount to subjugation of the non-white groups), there have been many subsequent racial episodes in the Union of South Africa. In 1952, thousands of Africans went to prison in non-violent demonstrations against governmental plans. There continue to be violent incidents from time to time, most of them localized up to now.

\* \* \*

Racial feelings often run especially high when the residential pattern of a neighborhood begins to change. In 1949, bombings wrecked the new homes of certain Negro citizens in Birmingham, Alabama—citizens who had dared to build good houses in an unoccupied area. In 1950, threats and violence attended the efforts of Dr. Percy Julian, world-famed Negro chemist, to move into a home he had purchased in a fashionable suburb of Chicago. Dr. Julian was forced to hire private guards to protect his property. In 1951, an apartment building in Cicero, another Chicago suburb, was wrecked by mobs because an apartment in it had been rented to a

Negro. In Miami Beach in December, 1951, bombs were thrown at Jewish synagogues and a new housing project for Negroes was seriously damaged. In Fort Worth, Texas, in September, 1956, a mob attacked the house of a Negro family who had moved into a white residential zone, and police barricaded the street in order to restore order.

\* \* \*

Among the most publicized of the recent episodes involving race was the series of incidents that followed Miss Autherine Lucy's attempt to study at the University of Alabama. After a three-year legal fight, Miss Lucy was admitted to the university in February of 1956. An exaggerated amount of publicity attended the event, and the fact that she was escorted by a police officer created an unusual atmosphere from the beginning. Student demonstrations, with some participation by other forces in the community, occurred immediately, and after three days of classes Miss Lucy was suspended from the university on the grounds of safety. When the Federal Court in Birmingham ordered her reinstatement a few weeks later, she was expelled for having made certain charges against the university administration.

While the Lucy case came to be very complicated, its most striking feature appears to have been the fact that trouble had not been anticipated adequately, despite Miss Lucy's police escort, and there was no concerted strategy for meeting it. This lack of preparation was shown particularly by religious leaders on the campus. A statement calling for tolerance, respect for fellow human beings, and regard for law, order, peace, and decency was adopted, but little else appears to have been done.

\* \* \*

These various incidents illustrate, in diverse ways, certain facets of the revolution that has been taking place in race relations and the status of colored peoples in the last few years. Many other dramatic instances could be cited: general strikes in Southern Rhodesia, riots in Uganda, the Mau Mau uprising in Kenya, a general strike in Mombasa, a massive revolt against French rule in Madagascar in 1947-48 (with between sixty thousand and a hundred thousand Malagasy losing their lives from all causes), the expulsion of most Western Europeans and Americans from Communist China, revolts in French Indochina and North Africa.

As these episodes indicate, the problem of race in the modern world is one of great variety and complexity. Each local community tends to think of the problem concretely in terms of its local pattern. But the local concerns vary immensely. They focus on Negro-white relations in the American South. They involve relations between whites, Mexicans, and Indians in the Southwest; whites and people of Oriental background on the

West Coast; "old stock" Americans, Puerto Ricans, and other new groups in New York City; West Indians and the British in London; the Chinese and majority groups throughout the nations of Southeast Asia; and so on indefinitely. There are certain similarities among all situations involving intergroup tension, but the local particularities cover a wide range.

It is also perfectly clear that the way in which any racial minority is treated anywhere in the world is no longer exclusively the business of the dominant group in one community or area. No important racial problem can be kept merely a local or regional problem, nor can measures to meet it be left solely in the hands of those most immediately involved. Hitler's massacre of Jews in Germany quickly came to be an important issue in many other countries. If the Union of South Africa has race riots, the entire continent quivers and the pulsations are heard around the world. Whenever a racial incident occurs in the United States, hundreds of millions of non-whites in Asia and Africa have their doubts about American democracy increased; it is notorious that an American speaking in either of those continents is likely to be questioned vigorously about the racial situation in his own country. In a revolutionary world, a dramatic instance of racial injustice becomes a powerful weapon in the world struggle. The treatment of neighbors at home becomes an important issue in dealing with nations abroad. In an interde-

10

pendent world, race relations anywhere have become the concern—the legitimate concern—of people everywhere.

An example of courageous action toward improvement of race relations likewise attracts world-wide attention. The action of the Supreme Court of the United States in 1954 that declared segregation in the public schools to be unconstitutional was acclaimed very widely in other nations. Even the Afrikaans-language press in the Union of South Africa gave extensive attention to it, while generally denying that the situation in the Union permitted movement in any similar direction. *Die Burger* concluded that the decision marked a complete transformation of American attitudes toward race relations within one generation, saying: "Just as in the case of the other Anglo-Saxon great power, Britain, a previously comparatively minority conception has within a short time become an active, fighting national ideology." This newspaper surmised that the change in America was due largely to the fight for world leadership against the Soviet Union.

In contrast, when Emmett Till, aged fourteen, was murdered in Mississippi because he allegedly whistled at a white woman, and the two white men widely considered to have been guilty were acquitted to the accompaniment of cheers in the courtroom, America's prestige in the remainder of the world suffered great damage. It was to be expected that the Communist press would make a great deal of the Till case, and it did so. Typical of many statements was that of *Das Freie Volk* in Dusseldorf, East Germany:

The life of a Negro in Mississippi is not worth a whistle. This verdict is again a sign of American Democracy. Knowing that in the U.S. every hysterical woman can send a Negro to the electric chair by claiming that she was insulted, it is not surprising that until now no white man was ever sentenced to death in Mississippi because he killed a Negro. Dulles and the other roving preachers of American democracy and freedom who babble about the "American way of life" and who want to make us their satellites, have thrown a heavy veil over such freedom and democracy.

But the reaction was by no means confined to the Communist publications; it was universal and included adverse comments from people of every shade of political outlook. Sharp questions were raised by non-Communists about the moral right of the United States to proclaim herself a champion of freedom and of oppressed peoples. A Paris newspaper, *Le Populaire,* observed:

The problem is the eternal problem of colonialism, which is a manifestation of the eternal problem of racism. Colonialism is a problem in France, or was yesterday in Great Britain, whose colonies are overseas. The essential difference is that the United States has its colony in the very interior of the country, while a third kind of empire, the USSR, has it on the borders. . . . Not too many Frenchmen have the right to give lessons to Americans in this area. However, certain Americans have a tendency to give lessons to others before having swept before their own door.

America's vulnerability is heightened, of course, by the contest with Russia for world leadership. That contest is not simply a power struggle, and it could not be settled by economic, political, or military measures alone. An equally important struggle for freedom and social justice is underway, and for the minds and loyalties of vast multitudes of people. Russia professes to be a revolutionary force to liberate the oppressed and to elevate the underprivileged of the earth. She has already all but succeeded in convincing many non-white peoples that she is their champion against the imperialism and chauvinism of the Western powers. Only the widespread suspicion that "liberation" by Communists may mean a new kind of imperialism, or the fate suffered by Hungary in 1956, has prevented her from even vaster influence in Asia and Africa. If she succeeds in isolating Western Europe and the Western hemisphere from the remainder of the world, she will have largely won the struggle for world leadership.

There are many parallels between the Soviet Union and the United States in regard to the treatment of racial groups. Both have fundamental traditions of equality and legal safeguards of it. If the United States has its Declaration of Independence, Bill of Rights, and Fourteenth Amendment, the Soviet Union

13

has its Declaration of the Rights of Peoples of Russia and its Article 123 of the Constitution of 1936.[1] Both nations have a great many ethnic minorities and their multi-racial situations compel them toward tolerance. Both also have records of serious defection on occasion from the ideals they profess.

It is possible to argue with cogency that the character of the Russian state at the present time produces equal tyranny for all groups and prohibits genuine freedom for any. That argument is more impressive to Western Europeans and Americans than to Asians and Africans who have not had freedom for generations and who are more largely concerned with equality.

It is also possible to argue that the fundamental revolution of the modern period was that of the seventeenth and eighteenth centuries in Britain, France, and America, when the people of great nations won self-government, and that the latter-day Communist revolutions are a perversion of this genuinely liberal and

---

[1] The Declaration, promulgated immediately after the revolution in 1917, proclaims equality, sovereignty, and self-determination for the peoples of Russia, and the abolition of special privileges and the right of free development for the ethnic groups, of which there are nearly two hundred in Russia, with nearly 150 different languages or dialects.

Article 123 of the 1936 Constitution states: "Equality of rights of citizens of the U.S.S.R., irrespective of their nationality or race, in all spheres of economic, state, cultural, social and political life, is an indefeasible law. Any direct or indirect restriction of the rights of, or, conversely, any establishment of direct or indirect privileges for, citizens on account of their race or nationality, as well as any advocacy of racial or national exclusiveness or hatred and contempt, is punishable by law."

liberating revolution. But the argument is not very convincing unless the sons and daughters of those earlier revolutionaries keep their forebears' spirit and ideals vigorously alive on behalf of other peoples struggling to be free and equal. Because of their deep involvement in the colonial system, the principal nations of Western Europe have often been in the position of resisting the latter-day equivalents of their own earlier revolutions. Since the United States has found it necessary to make common cause with these nations against the threat of communism, she has sometimes seemed to be also an enemy of the newer nations, though her generous action in making independence effective for the Philippines in 1946 has been widely applauded, and her opposition to the occupation of the Suez Canal by the British and French in 1956 has won new respect in Asia and Africa.

In short, the question of race has become within the last few years one of the most pervasive and important questions in the world. This is no less true in America than elsewhere, though the centrality of racial issues is a very recent development. In the 1920's, American attention was devoted mostly to questions of war and peace and to the development of welfare capitalism. In the 1930's, in the midst of a vast depression and unemployment, attention shifted to industrial relations and to alternatives among economic systems. World War II absorbed most interest from 1939 to V-J Day.

There are many indications that racial questions have been uppermost in many American minds since 1947, when the President's Committee on Civil Rights published its famous report and made recommendations for change.

Expressions of this enlarged and intensified interest in race are to be found in many areas. Most college campuses and student groups can cite instances of vigorous attention to it, and often of forthright action. Innumerable radio and television forums have been devoted to the matter recently. Whereas it was difficult to locate a dozen first-rate books on race fifteen years ago, the number published recently has been so large as to defy coverage. The colleges and universities reflect the new concern in their curricula, with some sixteen hundred courses in race relations now available in American institutions. At the state and community levels, hundreds of commissions and committees on race relations, fair play, fair employment practices, and the like have been organized, on both voluntary and official bases. Agitation for Federal agencies has been unceasing.

Even the motion pictures, sensitive to the interests of the public, have reflected the trend. Though most of the "race movies" have revealed more about Hollywood than about Harlem and have been more sentimental than penetrating, for a time it appeared that a trip to the movies might prove to be a sugar-coated sociological expedition. First there was *Gentlemen's Agreement.* Then came *Pinky; Lost Boundaries; Home of the Brave; Intruder in the Dust; Cry, the Beloved Country,* and many more. Most were based on best-seller novels or plays about race. Sex still leads the field of drama, but race has been moving up fast.

However superficial much of the new interest may be, it is nevertheless a token of the fact that America is seeking both to define her own ideals more clearly and to find her place in the world. The older assumption that she could live her life in comparative isolation without taking into account a rapidly changing world is now generally discarded, though there are still occasional declarations that the nation or some section of it will do as it pleases, on race or some other issue. A statement of this kind represents a vestige of the old isolationist spirit, though those who make it may often be in other respects rather fervent and dedicated internationalists. Unless America can rather quickly make her racial practices express good conscience before the conscience of the world, she is not likely to retain the leadership so largely entrusted to her now, or even to retain her own self-respect.

# Chapter Two

# FANCIES AND FACTS ABOUT RACE

It is well known that accurate information will not in itself change attitudes or conduct. In order to achieve a new way of life, an individual or a nation must educate the heart and the hands as well as the mind. "He that complies against his will is of his own opinion still." And a man whose will has also been convinced may still be helpless unless his hands can find instruments with which to serve his new loyalties. For this reason it is often futile to "argue" with people about the question of race or to preach at them without exposing them to new emotional commitments and to different methods of procedure.

18

At the same time, it is equally true that lack of accurate information may lead to the distortion of real issues and may obscure the alternatives available. Whatever else it may be, prejudice is inadequately informed; it has been defined as "being down on what you are not up on." (Ambrose Bierce defined it as "a vagrant opinion without visible means of support.") Though the roots and psychological foundations of racial prejudice are rather obscure, it may perhaps be defined as a commitment to attitudes and actions toward other groups without adequate knowledge of the facts about race.

It has been said that Christian virtue includes the ability to read a table of statistics with imagination. Similarly, Christians who are interested in their fellow men need to read with understanding the conclusions reached by a vast amount of research during the last half century on the question of race, though the general results may now be rather well known to most educated people.

In 1906, a judge of the Court of Appeals in Kentucky delivered the following opinion:

The separation of the human family into races, distinguished no less by color than by temperament and other qualities, is as certain as anything in nature. Those of us who believe that all of this was divinely ordered have no doubt that there was wisdom in the provision. . . . There exists in each race a homogenesis by which it will perpetually reproduce itself, if unadulterated. Its

19

instinct is gregarious. As a check there is another, an antipathy to other races, which some call race prejudice. This is nature's guard to prevent amalgamation of the races.

The first reaction to these views on the part of sophisticated moderns would probably be that of branding them as ancient superstition or "from the dark ages." Actually, the judge was expressing a very modern, indeed a practically recent, view of human differences. The term "race," insofar as it has a strong biological reference and alleged scientific support, is a modern term. Racially self-conscious groups, in this same sense of the term, are largely a modern development.

Groups with different physical characteristics have existed from the earliest time of which we have knowledge—though it is generally assumed, with a good deal of supporting evidence, that they have represented variations from one original human stock. From early times biological kinships have been noted, and distinctive physical characteristics have been ascribed to various groups. But the use, with pseudo-scientific evidence, of general physical or psychological characteristics as a basis for discrimination against allegedly inferior racial groups appeared seldom, if ever, before unwarranted assertions were made by recent racial theorists.

Ethnocentrism, the tendency of a group to exalt itself and to disparage other groups, appears to have been perennial. But it has generally focused attention in earlier periods on religious integrity (as in the Old Testament conception of the Chosen People living faithfully under a Covenant), or language (as in the Old Testament test of ability to pronounce "shibboleth"), or presumed common ancestry (valued in filial or totemic rather than racial fashion), or common territory, or some other factor. Physical differences were sometimes noted—the Greeks could distinguish themselves from the Scythians and the Jews could recognize the difference between themselves and the Samaritans—but were generally of secondary importance.

There is almost no teaching about race, as currently understood, in the great religious literatures of the world or in the writings of classical and medieval philosophers. For example, the Bible knows the term "race" only as a contest of speed or endurance. It has scores of references to "blood," and holds it in awe, but as the seat of the soul, the principle of life, rather than as a physiological bond or distinction among men. The crowning affirmation about blood, in any event, is that "now in Christ Jesus you who once were far off have been brought near in the blood of Christ" (Ephesians 2:13).

There are innumerable references to nations, tribes, and tongues, and it is perfectly clear that the people of the Bible were aware of differences among groups. It is equally clear that they did not have the equivalent of the modern concept of race. Despite the lack of any equivalent, however, the Bible contains much teaching that can be applied to illumine and evaluate the modern concept, as will be seen.

Foundations for a later theory of racial superiority are to be found in classical thought, though the theory itself is not developed there. Thus Aristotle was certain "Some men are born free, others slaves. For the latter slavery is both expedient and right." But he did not suggest that any particular group belonged entirely in either category. Rather, those who are superior *in virtue* should be masters, whoever they are. He clearly rejects the assumption that slavery is legitimate if it results merely from law or conquest. He regarded "the Hellenic race" as superior in achievements to the peoples of Asia and Europe, but he seems to attribute this more nearly to geography than to biology.

The foundations of a theory of racial equality and equal rights are likewise to be found in antiquity. The Stoics believed in universal brotherhood, and early Christians introduced warmth into this concept through emphasis on love for one another. Alexander the Great promoted intermarriage between Greeks and barbarians and had a common policy for treatment of both. The Roman Empire extended Roman citizenship to many non-Romans, among them Paul, a Jew from Tarsus.

It was not until almost exactly one hundred years ago that a well-articulated theory of racial superiority

22

appeared in the world, in the writings of a French diplomat, Comte Arthur de Gobineau. By that time the era of colonial expansion had been under way for about three hundred years, and white Europeans had come into contact with, and generally had subdued, colored peoples in most parts of the world. But the theory of racial superiority did not arise in the first instance from consideration of the proper relationship of white to colored. It arose in an effort to differentiate between classes of white Europeans and to buttress a declining aristocracy.

One hundred and twenty-five years before de Gobineau, another French nobleman, Comte Henri de Boulainvilliers, had suggested that the French nobility was descended from Franks (Germans) who had conquered the native Gauls, or Celts. He argued that the Franks had been a superior people in that they were defenders of political liberty, and that overthrow of the feudal system over which they had presided, brought about by a combination of the kings and the descendants of the conquered natives, had led to despotism.

Within ten years after the appearance of this thesis in 1727 it had been proved to be historically inaccurate. But traces of the same kind of theory continued to appear from time to time. At length de Gobineau, who had traveled extensively on diplomatic missions and had picked up a great many superficial impressions at first hand, published between 1853 and 1855 a four-volume work entitled, *Essai sur l'Inégalité des races humaines.*[1] His aim was primarily political: to fight the rising democratic spirit in Europe and to preserve the nobility. He believed that every nation and civilization is built on a mixture of races, but insisted that the future of European civilization depended on the dominance of the Aryans (who would today be called Nordics). In the dedication of his book he wrote:

I was gradually penetrated by the conviction that the racial question overshadows all other problems of history, that it holds the key to them all, and that the inequality of the races from whose fusion a people is formed is enough to explain the whole course of its destiny. . . . I convinced myself at last that everything great, noble, and fruitful in the works of man on this earth, in science, art, and civilization, derives from a single starting-point . . . it belongs to one family alone, the different branches of which have reigned in all the civilized countries of the universe.[2]

De Gobineau was not trying to establish the superiority of any nation over others; he was attempting rather to shore up the nobility of all countries by identifying them as Aryans. It was a class doctrine that he was preaching—and also a personal one, as a study of his own family tree reassured him that he was among the elect. He was certain that unless the aristocrats could

[1] Volume I has been translated into English by Adrian Collins, under the title *The Inequality of Human Races.*
[2] From the author's Dedication. American edition: G. P. Putnam's Sons, 1915. Used by permission of William Heinemann, Ltd., London, copyright holder.

keep both their racial purity and their power, civilization would be doomed.

It hardly needs to be pointed out that de Gobineau used as a racial category a term, "Aryan," that pertains primarily to a family of languages, and that those who have spoken these languages have been of highly diverse nationalities and physical characteristics. His appropriation and misuse of the term have given it a wider currency than it would ever have gained as a linguistic classification.

Comforting as they might have been to the nobility, de Gobineau's theories had little influence in France. But they were ready made for the rising nationalism in Germany, with its burning desire for unification and dominance. Richard Wagner introduced the theories to his circle, and they were soon elaborated and given new applications by his son-in-law, British-born but German-naturalized Houston Stewart Chamberlain. The latter's two-volume book published in 1890-91, *Die Grundlagen des neunzehnten Jahrhunderts,*[1] idealized the "Teutonic race" (Germans) and proclaimed that the regenerative, creative abilities of the Teutons had been one of the chief forces underlying European culture. There could be no future for Europe, he warned, unless the racial purity of the Teutons could be restored

[1] Both volumes have been translated into English by John Lees, under the title, *The Foundations of the Nineteenth Century.* New York, Dodd, Mead and Co., Inc., 1912.

and their energies released under the guidance of a purified Teutonic religion.

Chamberlain did not offer a definition of race, and his description of the Teutons is more mystical than precise. He scoffed at physical characteristics as clues; one knows a racial kinsman by intuition and spiritual affinities. Thus he was able to include Dante (a brunet) and Luther (roundheaded) and even Jesus (declared to have been not a Jew but a mixed Israelite with elements of Teutonic infusion) among the Teutons. One can know a Teuton in particular by his capacity for total loyalty to a leader.

Chamberlain obviously was using racial theory in support of German national aspirations rather than of a particular social class. He added to de Gobineau's theory another element destined to be of great consequence, namely, the assertion that the Jews are a degenerate, disruptive race.

Chamberlain's book in turn was ready made for the developing situation in Germany. The Kaiser helped to distribute it widely, and it made many disciples. One of the latter was a young politician who came under the direct influence of Chamberlain, Adolf Hitler. After their meeting in 1923, Chamberlain wrote to Hitler: "At one stroke you have transformed the state of my soul. Germany's vitality is proved if in this hour of its deepest need it can produce a Hitler."

The remainder of the story is written in tragic pages

of history. Hitler adopted Chamberlain's views whole-
sale, and the chapter, "Nation and Race," of his own
political testament, *Mein Kampf,* reveals his indebtedness at point after point. Thenceforth it was only a
short road to the extreme anti-Semitism of Alfred Ro-
senberg and the enactment of anti-Semitism into a legal
code at the Nuremberg Congress of 1935, the expropria-
tion of Jewish property in 1936, the pogroms of 1938,
and the ultimate extinction of millions of the Jewish
people. It had all started as a set of theories advanced as
special pleading unsupported by reliable evidence, a
hundred years before. The power of ideas, even false
ideas, over subsequent events has seldom been demonstrated more eloquently.

The race theories of de Gobineau, Chamberlain, and
lesser associates have had their influence also in other
countries. Madison Grant, and Lothrop Stoddard after him, mediated them to the United States. Here
they were used principally to exalt the "older American
stock," who were declared to be Nordics, and to deplore
the newer immigrants, who were said to be non-Nor-
dics. It was insisted that the dilution of the older stock
by the newer immigrants must be stopped if America
were to fulfill her destiny. The obvious political measure toward that end was to stop further immigration, a
result largely achieved in 1924 when Congress passed
the first general measure to restrict immigration.

The Negro American, barely emerged from slavery,

was no special problem for Grant and Stoddard; they seemed simply to assume that he knew his proper place to be one of segregation and subordination, and that he would keep it. With the rise of Negro-white relations to the center of attention, a great many books, pamphlets, and even mimeographed leaflets have reproduced the central ideas of de Gobineau, Chamberlain, and Hitler, applying them specifically to the new area of tension and demanding a "white America." Indebtedness to the nineteenth century racial theorists may be quite unconscious in most instances, but reproduction of the central ideas is so exact as to leave no doubt as to their ultimate origin.

These notions about race have also been influential in other countries. They were important in all the movements led by those who sympathized with Hitler, such as the fascist group in Great Britain that was headed by Oswald Mosley. They continue to be potent in the Union of South Africa: it is reported that the Broederbond (Band of Brothers), a secret society including most of the leaders of the ruling Nationalist Party, studied *Mein Kampf* with care, and certainly some of the racial ideas held by Hitler are widely prevalent in party circles. (A former Minister of Native Affairs told the writer that physical characteristics are not the primary criteria for determining racial affiliation; rather, a racial kinsman is to be identified by a feeling of spiritual affinity. He did not mention Chamberlain,

and it is possible that he had never heard of him.) A
developed in South Africa, the theory of *apartheid* in
its purest form does not include an assertion of racia
inferiority or superiority, but only racial *differences*
that require total separation of the races if each is to
realize its fullest possibilities. Leaders of the Nationalist Party have said frequently, however, that this idealized version of the theory is not practicable, and in
effect the doctrine has been used to maintain white
supremacy.

As is evident from this brief summary of racial theory, the doctrine of race has been entangled with class
interests, national aspirations, slavery, and colonialism.
It has been a prime instrument in the hands of politicians in various countries, who have changed its content at will to suit their purposes. Most especially, it
became a world issue when employed by Hitler, who
used it against a group religious rather than racial in
character.

While the propagandists have been devising their
theories, careful scientists have been attempting to define race and racial differences. Doubtless this would
seem to most men in the street to be no difficult problem; except for residents of heavily-mixed communities
such as Harlem or Honolulu, common-sense observation would seem to suffice, with skin color being the obvious test. But scientists have been at the task for more
than a hundred years, and their skepticism appears to

have increased as they have gone along. At various stages they have reached results that seemed conclusive (as when, at the turn of the century, the shape of the head —or cephalic index—seemed a fairly adequate criterion), only to have subsequent research bring fresh doubt (as when studies by Franz Boas during the years of this century showed that the head form may be affected by environmental conditions rather than being fixed by heredity alone). At the present moment, most serious students of the question agree that "race" is almost a meaningless term as far as scientific knowledge is concerned.

There is no problem in defining race theoretically: a race would be a group of people having a common inherited breed, with enough peculiar hereditary features in common to differentiate them from other groups. Perhaps "common stock" would be a better term than race.

In the effort to discover racial differences nearly every aspect of bodily structure and function, and of mental aptitude and capacity, has been studied carefully by a series of investigators. The color of skin, hair, and eyes; the texture of the hair; the projection of the upper lip; the shape of the head; stature; the size of the cranium; the shape of the nose; the thickness of the lips; the age of sexual maturity; the distribution of blood types— all these and many more have been measured with precision for large numbers of people. (Even the pelvic index has been studied, and it has been concluded that this is a useful criterion for telling the difference between the sexes!) On the basis of such measurements, an average can be arrived at for a supposedly racial group, and also a range of variability within the group. But the differences within the group itself are generally greater than the difference between the average of that group and the average of another. That is, "racial" groups differ internally more than they differ from one another. Put another way, families differ more than races. As between any two groups there will be great overlapping with respect to any physical characteristic.

The same holds true for mental abilities. Intelligence tests of many kinds have been given to members of all racial groups. Their results have often been used to argue that the white race is mentally superior and the Negro inferior, with yellow people coming in between. It has now become clear, however, that no test of intelligence has yet been devised that can rule out such non-hereditary factors as education, social opportunities, and other environmental influences (including even the desire to make a good score on an intelligence test). Intelligence tests are useful for ascertaining comparative ability along certain lines among persons who have had approximately the same environment and opportunities; their results are misleading if used to impute differences in hereditary endowment between groups of unequal background. Intelligence as measured by such tests has been shown actually to improve as individuals move into a more stimulating situation, as from an isolated rural community to a vigorous urban center. In any event, the matter of averages and internal variations enters the picture again; every racial group has its quota of brilliant people and stupid people, of gifted artists and clods, and racial groups resemble one another more in their intellectual capacities than they differ. All have languages, all can reason, all can love and hate.

The problem is that of finding sharp lines of division among actual human beings, when enough people are taken into account. In the abstract it is possible to divide mankind into three major groups; white, yellow, and black, or Caucasoid, Mongoloid, and Negroid. It is also possible to describe the physical characteristics considered to be typical of each of these groups, and to find a certain number of people who exemplify most of them. But the percentage of people who can be classified precisely will diminish as the number of required characteristics or the number of people under observation increases. The number of marginal, or in-between, cases will become as great, or even greater, than the "typical" representatives.

Suppose, for example, that a thousand people who classify socially as "white" were picked up at random and brought into a laboratory for careful study. On testing their skin color against a chart it would become apparent that they range from pinkish (or even albino) white to a rather dark brown. Many "white" people actually have darker skins than a great many people who classify socially as Negroes. In size of skull they range from pinheads to massive brows. In color of eyes and hair they vary greatly. Some have narrow heads and others round. Some are tall, some short. If given an intelligence test some would be too stupid to complete it, and others might be near genius. And so on: the more factors taken into account, the smaller would be the group of people corresponding to the stereotype (that is, usual conception or "fixed idea") of "the white race," and the greater would be the overlapping with stereotypes of the other races.

The same kind of result would be obtained by applying similar tests to large numbers of persons from other racial groups. If such tests were the basis for putting people into racial categories, the existing racial groupings in society would be altered drastically.

If it is suggested that ancestry rather than physical characteristics is the crucial point, the question of racial differences remains difficult. From the earliest times, there has been commingling of different groups, and there has probably been more in Europe and America than elsewhere. There are no unmixed races in the world. The mingling in America has included a large amount of intermating between white and Negro, so that a minority of Negro Americans are now of unmixed African descent. It is by no means certain that all white Americans are of unmixed European descent. Even if they were, it must be remembered that European descent is itself highly mixed. It is estimated, for example, that twenty-five million Jews (a group of non-European origin) have disappeared into the general non-Jewish population of Europe since the days of the Roman Empire—it would be extraordinary if Hitler himself did not have Jewish ancestors.

There is no evidence that the mingling of the races has produced deterioration of the human stock. Careful studies have been made of a number of hybrid groups, resulting from such mixtures as Boer-Hottentot, Japanese-Hawaiian, Maya-Spaniard, and so on. In most instances the hybrid group appears to be as strong—and in several instances stronger—physically and mentally as either of the parent strains. The old superstition that crossbreeding causes loss of fertility[1] is not supported by evidence from the Boer-Hottentot mixture, which averaged 7.7 children per family in the fifth generation after intermarriage.

These points are not made as an argument in favor of intermarriage. Fear that intermarriage will follow increased contact between the races is a palpable fact in certain parts of the world, and there is nothing to be

[1] This superstition helps to explain the adoption of the term "mulatto," derived from the same stem as "mule." It was assumed that the mulatto, like the mule, would be sterile.

gained by ignoring it or designating it a "red herring." The problem is that of getting the delicate question into proper perspective. Apparently there is no natural aversion to intermating, as is sometimes alleged; the historical record clearly indicates that sex does not necessarily draw racial lines. Nor does there seem to be any significant desire or compulsion toward intermarriage: in those American states that have not forbidden miscegenation by law the ratio of interracial marriages has been extremely low. An interesting example comes from a study made by Professor John H. Burma in California:[1] in the thirty months after the nullification of an anti-miscegenation statute in 1948, only one half of one per cent of all the marriages in polyglot Los Angeles County were interracial in character; only about one fourth of these involved Negroes, and about two thirds involved non-Mexican whites.

Serious social and psychological problems attend interracial marriages in many parts of the world, and often affect especially the social acceptability of children of such unions. A poignant example is found in the plight of the "butterfly babies" in Japan—the offspring of American GI's and Japanese girls. The Japanese government has undertaken to win public acceptance for them, but they are sometimes segregated or even abandoned. Their difficulties arise from social attitudes,

[1] "Research Note on the Measurement of Interracial Marriage," in *The American Journal of Sociology*, Vol. LVII, pp. 587-589 (May, 1952).

however, rather than from congenital inferiority or deficiency. As a panel of scientists assembled by UNESCO in 1950 put it: "There is no evidence that race mixture as such produces bad results from the biological point of view. The social results of race mixture whether for good or ill are to be traced to social factors." [1]

The more deeply one delves into the matter of race, the more confusing the picture becomes. This confusion is reflected among the scientists themselves: the number of races arrived at by the various scholars ranges from three or four to at least thirty-four. When those who have studied the facts most carefully are in such disagreement, and are almost unanimous in questioning the possibility of drawing racial lines clearly, it behooves the rest of us to tread lightly. Indeed, the UNESCO specialists assembled in 1950 proposed that the word "race" be discarded and that the term "ethnic group" be used instead.

The question of racial superiority is a still further question, of course, involving standards of value that are not in themselves subject to scientific validation. Superior in what way? Superior for what? Is brown a nicer shade than white? Is straight hair more becoming than curly hair—many Negro women think so, but many white women disagree, as the traffic in "permanents" will attest. Tall stature is a great advantage in viewing a parade or playing basketball but can be quite

[1] *What Is Race?*, p. 79. Paris, UNESCO, 1952.

a handicap to a person in a Pullman or in a shooting war.

The appeal to historical progress in support of white superiority also involves standards of value and a very careful selection of historical data. Great civilizations flourished in China and around the Eastern Mediterranean among dark-skinned people when Europe was still inhabited by barbarians. From the perspective of Greek civilization in the fourth century before Christ, Aristotle wrote: "Those who live in a cold climate and in Europe are full of spirit, but wanting in intelligence and skill; and therefore they keep their freedom, but have no political organization, and are incapable of ruling over others." In time, the Europeans proved Aristotle to have been wrong, and they spread out to rule nearly the entire world. In the process they damaged or destroyed the promising beginnings of non-European cultures, and at the same time they borrowed widely from the cultures of those they subjugated. Because of its technical superiority, Western culture is now being imitated widely by non-white peoples, and it may be that they will improve on it in time.

In short, the example of great nations and civilizations of the past that rose to dominance and then declined should prevent the notion that a group is naturally superior in ability merely because it is dominant at a given moment. It has been observed that history is rather like a horse race and that the ultimate winner, if there is to be one, is in doubt until the finish.

In any event, there seems to be no direct relation between race and culture, or between race and the ability to build a great civilization. The Indian tribes of America were of the same general racial background, but they differed greatly in ways of life and social organization. The Japanese wrought a revolution in their society without changing their race. Given the proper opportunity, any racial group could acquire any culture, and any culture could be achieved and maintained by diverse racial groups. Culture is acquired, while race is hereditary.

*Chapter Three*

# THE ROOTS OF PREJUDICE

In the United States any individual who can be shown to have had even one Negro ancestor is classified as a Negro. But there is a common saying in Brazil, where distinctions are largely those of class rather than race: "A rich Negro is a white man, and a poor white man is a Negro." In the Panama Canal Zone racial lines are sharply drawn and intermarriage is forbidden by public opinion, while in the adjacent Republic of Panama such lines are very fuzzy and intermarriage is widely practiced. In South Carolina, where racial categories are of supreme importance, live some five thousand people who simply cannot be classified;

generally called "Brass Ankles," they regard themselves as white and are regarded by neighboring white people as part Indian or Negro—though they are increasingly making their way into the white community, even through intermarriage.

These examples—and hundreds could be given—indicate that racial lines actually drawn in a society are man made, rather than being the work of nature or of nature's God. They may correspond roughly with actual physical differences, but that question is of little importance as far as a particular individual is concerned: if a person is classified as a Negro in the United States he is treated as a Negro, even if his skin be whiter than that of most of his white fellow citizens. In Puerto Rico and Brazil and Hawaii, on the other hand, the observable physical differences are very largely ignored in nearly every aspect of life, including social contacts. And even in the United States the way in which a member of a particular group is treated is subject to great variation, depending on the local customs, traditions, and ideas.

Certain individuals find it possible to change from one racial group to another almost at will, though their heredity obviously does not change in the process. It has been responsibly estimated that somewhere between two thousand and twenty thousand persons who had been classified as Negroes "pass" into the white group on a permanent basis in the United States each year.

Exact figures on this phenomenon are impossible because the very essence of success in passing is complete secrecy. Doubtless a much larger number pass as whites on occasion in order to avail themselves of the superior advantages open to the more privileged group. The danger of atavism—a dark-skinned baby born to a person passing as white—is practically non-existent, despite the persistent belief in it.

"Race" becomes a convenient handle on which to hang all sorts of personal fears or social conflicts—political, economic, religious, or what not—rather than being a natural cause of conflict. The identity of a racial group is defined largely in terms of cultural notions and social practices rather than by biology. A British anthropologist tells of a British sailor who was asked to describe a "Dago." "Dagoes," he replied, "is anything wot isn't our sort of chaps."

The arbitrariness of racial distinctions is sometimes illustrated in statutory definitions of race. In 1954, the government of the Union of South Africa decided that a white man married to an Indian woman would henceforth be classified as an Indian, a white man married to a Chinese woman would be regarded as Chinese, and one married to a Malay woman as Malay.

Unofficial definitions can sometimes be even more confused. Some years ago, a private club in Florida, organized to operate a swimming pool, sought to draft a membership clause that would exclude both Negroes and Jews. Restriction of membership to "Christians" would not suffice, as Negroes might then seek admission. Restriction to "whites" was equally unsatisfactory, as Jews would not thereby be excluded. The clause finally adopted was, "Membership shall be open only to white persons of the Christian race."

Racial aversions and hatreds are likewise acquired socially rather than being the work of nature. We are not born with prejudices, but only with the potentialities for developing them. A great many people never develop *racial* prejudices at all, even where there is ample opportunity, and there are entire multi-racial societies where they are at a minimum—the examples of Puerto Rico, Hawaii, and Brazil have already been cited. Racial hatreds may be deliberately aroused for political or other purposes, as in Nazi Germany: the Jews of Germany had been rather thoroughly assimilated and accepted until a concerted effort was made to isolate and persecute them.

The roots of racial prejudice are not very well understood. Though there are many theories about the question, no one has been proved adequate. One theory emphasizes "social visibility": racial prejudice increases as the *number* of the minority group approaches that of the majority. Thus, it is argued, there is little prejudice against the Negro in New England because few Negroes are resident there; there is great prejudice in Mississippi because it is the one state in which the number of

Negroes approximately equals the number of whites. Or, there is prejudice against the Oriental on the West Coast but not in the South. One body of Southern religious leaders went so far recently as to assert that prejudice would decline in the South simply because so many Negroes were moving to the North.

While the fear of being engulfed by a group regarded as inferior may be a factor underlying prejudice in certain situations, it is by no means as decisive or inevitable as is generally supposed. Though the degree of prejudice is hardly measurable, there appears to be no proportional relation between it and the numerical ratios; the whites of South Africa, outnumbered three to one by the Bantu (who comprise nearly all of the Africans in the Union), are not necessarily three times as prejudiced as those of Mississippi. In any event, whites comprise only 2 per cent of the population of Jamaica and only 40 per cent of that of Brazil, but they show little racial prejudice despite the numerical superiority of the colored groups.

Another theory takes an historical point of view. It seeks to explain the rise of prejudice and racial discrimination in terms of the peculiar history of a particular region. For example, it is argued that the racial attitudes of Southern whites in the United States are a residue of the slavery system and of the bitterness engendered during the Reconstruction period after the Civil War. There can be no doubt that an illumination of

43

"how people got that way" can help in the understanding of their present attitudes. But the implication of inevitability in the historical process should be avoided: the history itself was made up of human choices that could have been made otherwise in many instances.

It is important, also, that history should be understood accurately rather than rewritten to justify later developments. Thus, it has now been made clear by Professor C. Vann Woodward [1] that social relations between Southern whites and the emancipated Negroes were rather informal and congenial in the South during the days of Reconstruction, and that the present patterns of rigid segregation were deliberately devised only in the last decade of the nineteenth century and the first years of the twentieth.

It is very popular to attribute prejudice simply to ignorance. There can be no doubt that racial groups living in the same community are often misinformed about one another; each tends to build up a mythology about the others in the effort to support or rationalize its own position. In 1947, the National Opinion Research Center took a poll among Americans representing many groups to determine their feeling about the loyalty of Americans of Japanese ancestry during World War II; 66 per cent of the people questioned believed that at least some, if not all, had been spies for the Japanese

[1] In *The Strange Career of Jim Crow*. New York, Oxford University Press, 1955.

44

Government during the war. The truth was, according to the FBI, that not one person of Japanese ancestry, whether American citizen or alien, living in the United States or Hawaii, was convicted of either espionage or sabotage.

Earlier, in 1944, the same research organization had asked whether Negroes have the same chance as white people to make a good living in the United States. Forty-four per cent of the white people answered in the affirmative, but 85 per cent of the Negroes thought that opportunities were unequal. Sixty per cent of the Southern whites thought chances were the same. Most interesting of all, Gunnar Myrdal found, in his study[1] of Negro-white relations in America, that white fears about the Negro and the latter's actual desires were almost exactly in inverse relation. Whites were most concerned to bar the Negro sexually and least unwilling to let him have a decent job; Negroes were most interested in economic opportunity and least concerned about intermarriage.

However widespread ignorance may be, and however much it may help to buttress a pattern of discrimination already established, there is some doubt as to its role in causing prejudice to arise in the first place. Ignorance would seem to lead more largely to indifference than to active aversion. By the same token, it is quite clear that enlightenment alone will not always remove prejudice.

[1] *An American Dilemma*. New York, Harper and Bros., 1944.

Economic competition is often judged to be a source of prejudice. Lower income whites have often feared the competition of Negro labor at a still lower wage level. One historic study found a relationship between the price of cotton and the occurrence of lynching in an American Southern county, without suggesting that the price of cotton was solely responsible for the phenomenon of lynching. In the Philippines there is acute resentment on the part of Filipinos against the virtual monopoly over trade held by Chinese merchants. It could be pointed out also that both the American South and South Africa are in some respects rather poor regions (despite the latter's fabulous production of gold and diamonds), and that the competition for available income is intensified accordingly.

Beyond question, economic pressures have influenced race relations, sometimes almost decisively. When workers from a minority group have been imported as cheap labor or as strike-breakers, great bitterness has often been aroused among workers of the dominant group. Anti-Semitism generally is influenced, legitimately or not, by the economic prowess of the Jews. But it has not been demonstrated that economic competition always produces racial prejudice: the struggle for a livelihood is present in Brazil, but there is little racial feeling.

In recent years, a great deal of attention has been given to psychological explanations of race prejudice. One well-known theory is based on the argument that certain types of personality, authoritarian in structure, are inherently prone to prejudice. Other studies have called attention to the influence of fear, frustration, aggression, guilt, projection, and other psychological processes. The "scapegoat" theory has been widely accepted: we compensate for some failure or weakness in ourselves by blaming some weaker group conveniently at hand. It has been seriously suggested that intolerance can be overcome in some individuals only by prolonged psychoanalysis and therapy.

Psychologists and psychiatrists have made valuable contributions in clarifying the mechanisms of prejudice and its roots in certain individuals. But personality can hardly be divorced from the types of influences described in the preceding paragraphs; it is formed in a matrix of social and cultural forces, even though we may grant that an individual at birth has tendencies toward being a certain type of person. He may become so prejudiced a person, of course, that only psychiatric help, if that, can make him tolerant again.

A final type of theory gives specific emphasis to social conditioning, and might be designated as a sociological explanation of prejudice. Though it takes many forms, this approach generally centers attention on the ways in which a person becomes a member of an "in-group" or "we-group" that defines itself in part by deprecation of other groups. An early American sociologist called this process the development of "consciousness of kind." It is not so much that birds of a feather naturally flock together; young humans are taught by parents, home life, and countless other environmental influences to be "of a feather." Born without a feeling of racial identity or superiority, and playing naturally in early years with anybody who will play, they acquire the attitudes prevalent in the family and community. Beliefs and attitudes thus come to be self-perpetuating, though they are carried at a given moment by individuals and groups who are theoretically free to change or discard them.

Doubtless all these theories need to be kept in mind in an effort to understand racial intolerance. Prejudice, like the definition of race, is infinitely variable, both as to the sources from which it springs and as to the forms in which it manifests itself.

By a curious but understandable reaction, a minority being discriminated against often develops a picture of itself resembling that held by the dominant group. Because they were expected to act as inferior, many Negro Americans have become obsequious, sometimes as a technique to avoid trouble but also on occasion because the white notion has invaded the Negro mind. The most exaggerated example of this adoption of a prescribed role was seen in a small group of German Jews who became fervent Nazis and adopted as their slogan the equivalent of "Down with us!" Many Negroes feel uneasy or shocked when a member of their group violates taboos. The same kind of psychological reaction is observable in woman's acceptance of man's concept of her status and role. Self-disparagement often develops in a minority group because of discrimination.

It is a moot question as to whether minority status can lead to greater creativity. It has been argued that the Jews in a great many situations have been stimulated to outstanding literary and musical accomplishments because of persecution, and it is obvious that America's best-known music is Negro music interpreted very largely by Jews. It may be that the necessity on the part of members of a minority to work harder in order to accomplish as much as members of the majority has led them to accomplish more in the end. But the generalization is dangerous and lacks conclusive evidence. It is like the old dictum that a poet produces poetry from the pain in his stomach; while suffering may help to evoke poetry, it would be foolish public policy and callous private conduct to starve poets.

Alongside and contradictory to the tendency to reflect the dominant group's view of itself, a minority often builds up its own sense of group pride, sometimes defensively and sometimes militantly. As the Negro American has become better educated and more keenly aware of the discrimination against him, he has also tended to take greater pride in his own group. There is probably less passing from the Negro to the white group than formerly. While the right of integration into the larger community is doubtless desired by most Negroes, the practice of integration even when possible is not always fully carried out. Desegregation of the public schools in Baltimore, Maryland, was undertaken in the fall of 1954, with Negro children being given their choice of schools. It is reported that only 2½ per cent chose to enter schools that had previously been all white. If every church in America invited any sincere Christian to join in its worship, without any barrier of race or color, it is unlikely that patterns of church attendance would change greatly for many years. But the attitudes of many people toward the churches and of the churches toward themselves would change profoundly.

Whatever the sources of racial prejudice, its power and its cost are incalculable. If it is stimulated at times by economic factors, it can also override economic considerations almost to the point of ruin. Many Southern unions jeopardized their own wage scales for years by exclusion of the Negro from membership. Though authorities disagree as to the comparative cost of integrated and separate-but-equal education, it has been estimated that thirty million dollars would be saved in the state of Missouri alone (exclusive of Kansas City) by a completely integrated public school system, as over against a separate-but-equal system, and comparable savings would doubtless be possible elsewhere; yet there are many proponents of the more costly alternative.

Considerations of race can take precedence over commitment to public education, as is currently being demonstrated in some Southern states. They can result in the suspension or denial of elementary civil rights, as in mass arrests of those who speak out against official racial policies in South Africa. They can take precedence over national patriotism, as in the refusal to allow members of a minority group to bear arms in the defense of the country or to have wartime jobs consonant with their ability. They can be more powerful even than religious commitment: although surveys have shown that most religious leaders in the American South, and some in South Africa, are uneasy about the reconciliation of segregation with their Christian faith, the churches remain segregated.

The cost of prejudice to individual personalities is beyond all measurement. It is obvious that it thwarts aspirations and often produces bitterness in those against whom it is directed. But it also can pervert and distort the personality that is prejudiced, sending it in the direction either of monomania or schizophrenia. Generous impulses are often frustrated, and kindred but exaggerated prejudice in others can lead to results that cause a sense of guilt and shame. Instead of living freely in a wide world of two and a half billion human beings, most of them so intensely interesting that the variety of personalities is a fascinating spectacle, one comes to live by suspicions and fears and to draw the imprisoning circle of fear and avoidance ever tighter as its perimeter is threatened by those regarded as inferior.

*Chapter Four*

## THE VARIABILITY OF CASTE

However elusive the sources and incalculable the cost of racial prejudice, the social results are easily ascertained. It creates and in turn is sustained by a system of caste. In contrast to class lines, which are more or less flexible and can be overcome by individuals, caste represents an attempt to freeze various levels of status, opportunity, and privilege in a society. Inherited and inescapable biological characteristics, whether physical or mental or both, are ascribed to the various castes, and there is generally some notion of untouchability.

The submerged caste is always regarded as inferior

and is literally submerged: its ceiling of privilege must be lower in certain respects than the floor of the dominant group. There can be no recognized transfer from the lower to the higher caste without misrepresentation of origin. There may be classes within each caste, with individuals arranged in layers according to their shades of color, their attitude toward the stronger caste or toward their own, and other such criteria. But the caste line itself is regarded as inviolable.

The caste system of any community is defended by a set of myths that are used to justify the restrictions, different levels of privilege, and practices of etiquette that separate the various groups from one another. Caste rules are often quite inconsistent with the functional relations of the groups involved. Many white persons will not eat with a Negro but are quite willing, even eager, to have their food prepared by one. Many white people are unwilling to send their children to school with Negro children but do not question having a colored nurse for the baby.

Since the relationships of racial groups are defined socially and culturally, as already noted, the patterns vary greatly from time to time and place to place. By the same token, racial barriers tend to be movable screens rather than stationary walls, though racists usually consider them inexorably a part of nature.

Many types of interracial relations and racial barriers might be analyzed with profit and with growing insight:

white settlers and Kikuyus in Kenya; colonial officers and Africans in West Africa; Europeans and aborigines in Australia; Englishmen and West Indians in Great Britain; Puerto Ricans and continental Americans in the United States; castes in India; Japanese and refugees and G.I. babies in Japan.

Perhaps it will be most rewarding, however, to compare situations in the two places where race has come to be most important—the Union of South Africa and the Southern region of the United States. The analysis of each will be confined to relations between the white group and the principal non-white group in the population.

The race barriers in these highly dissimilar societies reveal many common features, though they have been erected as a result of quite different histories. The barriers are higher and more completely impenetrable in South Africa than in the Southern region of the United States, but basically they are much the same. Physical movement of the Africans is severely limited by an elaborate system of passes and laws about migration from native territories; travel by the Negro in the South is restricted in terms of convenience and dignity. There is residential segregation in both places. It is enforced in the United States largely through social pressure and real estate covenants. In South Africa segregated "locations" or townships near the white cities and a system of native reservations have been established by law.

Barriers to equality of opportunity for employment have tumbled rapidly in America (taken as a whole) in the past fifteen years, but it is still impossible for most Africans to hold jobs requiring any genuine skill.

Access of the African to education has always been limited, and the situation at present is confused and controversial. In the past, the government has been content to leave the education of African children largely in the hands of the missions, which in the course of 150 years have built up a system ranging from the nursery school to the college. These schools have been supported by contributions from the people, help from the sending churches, and subsidies in some provinces from the territorial governments. The Bantu Education Act, which has been in force since 1955, has in effect transferred control of state-aided schools from the missions to the government, with administration largely in the hands of community organizations. The government claims that one of the purposes of the law is to give education to a larger number of African children, an argument that has appeal, since the resources of the missions permitted them to give educational opportunities to only one third of the African children. However, many observers see the law as a move to make the schools an instrument of white supremacy by freezing education at the level the government thinks suitable for the African. In short, they feel that its real purpose is to give Africans enough education to make them useful workers in inferior positions but not enough to provide for their all-around cultural development. The Negro in the United States, in the so-called "separate but equal" schools, has also suffered from the limitations of second-class education.

The African is completely excluded from political participation; the Southern Negro increasingly exercises political rights, though often fearfully and under some pressure. Access to other social privileges—markets, clubs, public assemblies, public services—is limited and often non-existent for the African; it is still limited, but increasingly available, for the Southern Negro insofar as public facilities are concerned. Private social groups, such as clubs, are of course still separate for whites and Negroes.

A comparison of these two social systems reveals other interesting similarities: (1) In each place racial theories were imported and adapted to justify local measures. (2) Though the numerical ratios of the dominant and submerged groups differ—one to three in South Africa, not more than one to one in any Southern state taken as a whole—there is in each instance a genuine fear on the part of the white group that it will be diluted and finally overwhelmed biologically and politically. (3) Fear of economic competition from the non-white worker is present in each situation. (4) The dominant groups have many striking characteristics in common: both by tradition elevate religion to a central place in the community and quote the Bible frequently; both make a great deal of family ties and of the dominance of the father in the household; both have a strong sense of cultural distinctiveness and identity (Boer nationalism and Southern regionalism); both have a sense of physical isolation; both are still basically rural peoples despite the recent growth of great cities, and both are still suspicious of urban groups and views; each has traditions of a plantation or semi-plantation economy requiring cheap labor; both were defeated in a crucial war by the superior might of racial fellows, and the consequent resentment may have been transferred in part to a presumably inferior group close at hand. (5) In each society there is a dissenting group, as far as racial policies are concerned, within the dominant group itself: in South Africa, many English-speaking South Africans and a few Dutch Reformed pastors; in the United States, many Southern liberals and probably a majority of the non-Southern whites.

There are also significant differences between the two situations: (1) The Negro's gifts, like those of many other groups, have helped to mold the American culture, and the Negro American has no separate culture; the cultures of the various Bantu tribes still differ immensely from that of the Europeans. (2) Though there are nearly a million colored people (i.e., people of mixed ancestry) in South Africa, miscegenation is far more advanced in the United States, with perhaps less

57

than 30 per cent of the Negroes being of pure African descent. (3) The Negro American community is far better organized and has stronger, more vigorous leadership than the African. (4) The basic constitutional principles and general traditions in America point toward equality among men, while those in South Africa point toward racial separation at best or subjugation of the Bantu at worst. (5) There has never been a pattern of lynching in South Africa. It has now almost disappeared in America, after having been a major feature of race relations for more than fifty years.

Racial discrimination is more extensive and more completely established in the American South and in South Africa than anywhere else in the world. As the foregoing comparison of these two societies would suggest, the differences between patterns of racial relationships are quite as significant as the similarities. In each case a group superior in power has imposed its will on a weaker group, but the devices employed have varied notably. Extension of the analysis to include other nations would increase the range of variability in race patterns still further.

This variability attests to the fact that caste is not a fixed, immutable phenomenon, but that race relations are contrived by man and are continually changing. The drawing of racial lines, the sources of racial prejudice, and the actual patterns of race relations—all these are relative in time and place, and yesterday's accepted order becomes tomorrow's battleground. As in all areas of human relations, change is not only possible; it is inevitable.

The variability of the caste system is nowhere better illustrated than in the United States. Probably the most dramatic changes in the entire history of race relations have occurred in this country in the last one hundred years, and especially in the last twenty years. Their nature and extent can best be depicted in terms of the achievements and widening opportunities of the Negro American. A Negro publisher summed up the story with understandable exaggeration: "Every Negro is a Horatio Alger. . . . His trek up from slavery is the greatest success story the world has ever known."

For a time after the abolition of slavery, Negroes enjoyed extraordinary privileges, including that of holding high public office even in the South. Segregation in public schools was established in the South during Reconstruction, and the Negroes themselves withdrew from mixed churches rather than accept segregated status inside them. As had been the case during the days of slavery, the Negro was generally regarded as inferior, and most Negroes were illiterate. But very few laws existed to restrict freedom of access, without segregation, to transportation, public facilities, and the like, and this situation continued to prevail for the most part for twenty years after the withdrawal of Northern troops in 1877.

The Jim Crow system in the South—and in particular respects in some other sections of the nation—was instituted by law and custom at the turn of the twentieth century. It is not, as is often supposed, the age-old pattern of race relationships in the South; arrangements were quite different under the cotton-slavery-planation system from 1810 to 1860, and again quite different during the post bellum period from 1865 to 1895. A number of developments conspired in the 1890's to overthrow the moderate attitude toward the Negro that had prevailed (except for the Ku Klux Klan and the rapid rise in the number of lynchings in the late 1880's) in the years since the Civil War. The Populist movement, spurred on by economic depression, threatened the dominance of conservative political leadership. The Supreme Court in 1896 ruled that facilities for Negroes might be separate if they were equal in quality—a doctrine destined to prevail in the decisions of the Court until 1954. In 1898, the Court permitted the disfranchisement of the Negro. Negro leadership itself was confused and unable to offer effective resistance: in 1895, Booker T. Washington, already an outstanding leader, made his famous Compromise Address in Atlanta, saying to the white people: "In all things that are purely social we can be as separate as the fingers, yet one as the hand in all things essential to mutual progress."

These and other events set the stage for the extensive web of legislation by state legislatures and town authorities by which the system of segregation was defined and enforced. Legislative action was reinforced and extended, and to some degree stimulated in the first place, by informal and unofficial practices on the part of whites. By 1910, the pattern of segregation was firmly established in most areas of life. Judged before the Civil War by his qualities as a slave, the Negro was henceforth to be judged for decades by his ability to adjust to second- or third-rate conditions of life: to inferior wages, houses, schools, hospitals, railroad cars, hotels, hospital service, recreational facilities. Waiting rooms in railway stations had to be separate; so did ticket windows, toilets, and even cemeteries. Deprived of equal status and opportunity, the Negro in the South developed a complicated psychological mechanism to combine obsequiousness and the shreds of his integrity.

It should not be supposed that segregation was limited to the South or to the Negro. While the South was devising new methods to control the Negro, or "to keep him in his place" (as the expression came to be), the other regions of the nation were developing comparable methods for management of other minorities. Immigrants (especially Jews) in the East, Orientals in the West, Mexicans in the Southwest—all were welcomed as cheap labor and repudiated as equal human beings. The South built its segregated ghettos for Negroes at the edge of town; a similar result was achieved in Northern cities by the insertion of restrictive covenants in deeds to property. Southern universities barred Negroes; universities elsewhere often barred them too, from both student body and faculty, and established quotas for Jews. Barriers to full rights of citizenship for Negroes were matched by similar obstacles for Mexicans and Orientals. Everywhere in America the barriers went up; the old stock must be protected from the immigrant, the Christian from the Jew, the white people from the Negro. Regional differences in the treatment of racial minorities became less and less significant, and were largely matters of degree.

Despite the restrictions placed on him, the Negro continued to make remarkable progress in the evolution from slavery toward genuine independence. Illiteracy declined from about 95 per cent at the time of emancipation to less than 10 per cent. Though the amount spent for public education per Negro child was still only one third of that per white child in the South as a whole in 1940, the figure rose very rapidly thereafter, and by 1950, the average expenditure per Negro child was 58 per cent of that per white child. More than a hundred colleges were founded over the years for the higher education of Negroes, with boards of home missions in the forefront of the movement; 46,343 Negro students were enrolled in colleges by 1953-54. In economic possessions, the Negro rose from complete poverty to the ownership of several billion dollars of wealth in 1940 and an annual expenditure of at least two billion dollars. More than seventy thousand Negro business establishments were in operation by this latter year: retail stores, banks, insurance companies, newspapers, and many other types. Increasingly the Negro became urbanized and more widely dispersed in residence: by 1940, there were twelve American cities with more than a hundred thousand Negroes, and nine of them were outside the traditional South. The list of Negro accomplishments, in which whites both North and South had also a significant part, could be extended indefinitely.

The greatest revolution, however, has taken place in the last twenty years. This revolution has brought not only a remarkable improvement in the condition of the Negro; it has also wrought profound changes in his relations with the whites. When viewed in long perspective, one of the salient characteristics of this generation in the United States may be the fact that the walls of segregation have been torn down at a rapid rate. For the most part this has been effected thus far in non-violent fashion, with occasional mobs and riots receiving publicity out of all proportion to their importance in relation to the total picture.

So many changes have taken place that many pages would be required merely to list them. Negro baseball players have been admitted to the big leagues and Jackie Robinson and Don Newcombe have become heroes to the sand-lot gangs. This is very important; prejudice against immigrants was diminished by the fact that football and baseball players with unpronounceable names became heroes to the children and the public. A Negro, Dr. Ralph Bunche, has achieved one of the highest posts in international affairs, and has been awarded the Nobel Peace Prize. A number of college fraternities have defied their national organizations by admitting Negroes to membership. Segregation in the armed services has been eliminated. Lynching has virtually disappeared. In Washington, D. C., formerly a stronghold of discrimination, segregation has been abolished since 1954 in schools, theaters, restaurants, and playgrounds.

By a series of Supreme Court decisions, doors have been opened to Negroes that had been closed for fifty years. Decisions since 1940 have established the following principles: Negro teachers shall receive equal pay for equal qualifications and work; the right to vote in primaries shall not be restricted on grounds of race; segregation may not be used in interstate railroad dining cars or even on local buses; restrictive covenants in deeds to property shall not be enforceable in Federal courts; a state is obliged to furnish to qualified Negro applicants a graduate or professional education really equal to that available for whites; segregated treatment of a student after admission is unlawful; and (most momentous of all) segregation in public schools, parks, playgrounds, and golf courses is unconstitutional. These latter decisions, made in 1954 and 1955, reversed the doctrine of "separate but equal" opportunities followed by the Court itself since 1896. The Interstate Commerce Commission joined the trend by ruling in 1955 that racial segregation in interstate train and bus travel would no longer be permitted, with such facilities as waiting rooms also being included in the ruling.

The impact of the Supreme Court's rulings with regard to educational opportunities has brought changes so swiftly that any account of them is quickly out of date. The gap between Negro and white students in expenditures and capital outlays per pupil has rapidly narrowed in the Southern states and by 1954 had, in some instances, very nearly vanished. By 1956, more than one hundred, or nearly half, of the publicly-supported colleges that had been reserved for whites in the Southern and border states had opened their doors to Negroes, with the Lucy incident at the University of Alabama being the only instance of violence. Several hundred private colleges have admitted Negroes for the first time during the last decade, and several scores of them are in the Southern and border states. Estimates are precarious, but there are perhaps three thousand Negroes now studying in institutions of higher learning from which they were previously excluded, and more than one hundred predominantly white institutions now have Negro faculty members. Only five Southern states have refused thus far to begin desegregation of their tax-supported colleges and universities at any level.

Following the Supreme Court's ban in 1954 on segregation in the public schools, and its instruction to lower courts a year later that they should require "a prompt and reasonable start toward full compliance," desegregation has proceeded gradually but impressively. It has taken place thus far, as far as the Southern region of the nation is concerned, only in the various "border states" surrounding the traditional South, and in the District of Columbia. When schools opened in the fall of 1956, eight states remained almost entirely segregated. In the nine surrounding states and the District of Columbia, preliminary reports indicated that 723 school districts would be integrated and three thousand others would remain segregated for the time being. About 20 per cent of the districts had, therefore, been integrated in a three-year period. Integration was proceeding most rapidly in Delaware, Kentucky, Maryland, Missouri, Oklahoma, Texas, West Virginia, Kansas, Tennessee, and the District of Columbia: it had scarcely begun in the public schools of Alabama, Florida, Georgia, Louisiana, Mississippi, North Carolina, South Carolina, and Virginia.

Violence and mob action accompanied the efforts at integration in a few communities and made national headlines; in most situations the transition was made smoothly and received comparatively little attention. 't seemed probable that the movement toward integration would spread from the periphery deeper and deeper into the South, despite evasive tactics devised to resist it. Early in 1954, segregation in the public schools was required by law in seventeen states and the District of Columbia and permitted in four others; by 1956, the picture had altered drastically.

Supreme Court decisions regarding the political and civil rights of Negroes and other minorities have likewise had great effect. Though figures on registration and voting by racial groups are mostly guesswork, it has been estimated that 250,000 Negroes voted in the South in 1940, that 1,200,000 were registered in the region in 1952, and that the number voting there in 1956 may have reached 3,000,000. Much intimidation remains, but the Negro voters have now reached a position in which they could be the balance of power in elections in several states. This possibility has not escaped the notice of politicians in the North or South.

When haled before lower courts, the Negro is still often at a disadvantage as compared with the white defendant, but differential treatment appears to be declining, and it has practically disappeared in higher courts. The bitter epigram that "justice may be blind but not entirely color blind" has less and less evidence to support it.

In interstate transportation and access to other public facilities, the segregation of the Negro has either disappeared or suffered severe modification. Legal rulings are clearer than actual practice in such matters, and it is certain that a great deal of habitual discrimination remains in effect.

Vast changes have occurred in the economic status and opportunities of Negroes during the last fifteen years. Traditionally they have been confined largely to domestic service and agriculture; when they entered industry at all, it was generally at the level of unskilled employment, and opportunities for training and advancement were poor. During World War II, an unprecedented number of Negro workers were admitted to the factories. Hitherto barred from white-collar jobs that would bring them into contact with the general public—serving as clerks in department stores, front office secretaries and receptionists, and the like—they have now been admitted to such occupations very widely. The riots and boycotts that had been feared have failed to materialize.

As a result of these and other changes, including the general rise in prosperity, the economic status of the Negro is greatly improved. The two-billion-dollar annual purchasing power of 1940 has soared to an annual figure of approximately fifteen billion dollars. The average income of Negro wage and salary workers has increased both absolutely and in its ratio to that of the white worker, but in 1949 the average Negro family income was still only about half that of the average white family. In home ownership, however, the Negro is acquiring property at a faster rate than the white group.

The status of Negroes in the trade unions has also changed, and the unions for the most part are now admitting all qualified workers without discrimination. The CIO has been officially opposed to segregation in its unions from the beginning, and there are those who claim that this national movement has been one of the principal leaders in the fight to break down racial barriers in America. A number of the unions in the AF of L have had discriminatory practices, but several have changed their rules since 1940. The Railway Brotherhoods, by and large, have been slowest to admit Negroes, but there are now signs of change among them. There are a great many mixed union locals even in the South, where perhaps 700,000 Negroes are to be counted among the region's 2,750,000 union members.

This extended—but still too brief—analysis of the changing status and fortunes of the Negro in the United States during the last one hundred years is one of history's best illustrations that race relations are not fixed once and for all by differences in ability or by impregnable custom. They are the result of social forces and human aspirations; as such, they are capable of rapid change. It is not too much to say that a revolution has taken place, and is still proceeding, in race relations in the United States. There is good reason to believe that it will approximate the goal of full opportunity and unsegregated privileges for all citizens regardless of race, color, creed, or national origin. Some observers contend that the revolution is proceeding too rapidly at present; sometimes they are sincerely in favor of change at a slower pace, but frequently their argument is used to buttress the old regime for as long as possible. A great many whites are not yet ready for the concessions required of them. Some of the Negroes are not quite prepared for the new opportunities and relationships. But history seldom waits for the slowest. A revolution is under way; movement toward integration may be deflected temporarily in certain instances, but its eventual success is almost beyond question.

This is an issue with implications wider than the welfare of the people immediately concerned. Gunnar Myrdal urged:

> If America in actual practice could show the world a progressive trend by which the Negro became finally integrated into modern democracy, all mankind would be given faith again. . . . And America would have a spiritual power many times stronger than all her financial and military resources—the power of the trust and support of all good people on earth. *America is free to choose whether the Negro shall remain her liability or become her opportunity.*[1]

[1] *An American Dilemma,* by Gunnar Myrdal, pp. 1021-1022. New York, Harper and Brothers, 1944. Used by permission.

*Chapter Five*

# THE THEORY OF INTEGRATION

A society composed of several racial groups may choose among a number of philosophies as to the best method of dealing with differences. An individual has the same options.

The decision may be to *ignore differences*. Treat everybody as an individual. As far as groups are concerned, let them flow together naturally without any particular molding. This is the philosophy apparently accepted in the dictum that America is a melting pot: "We are Americans all and immigrants all."

This view has a certain appealing quality; it renounces racial prejudice and recognizes the essential oneness of mankind. It seems rather unrealistic, however, when translated into a policy of dealing with a situation where different groups actually do exist, each with its own self-consciousness and it own aims. It is the equivalent in race relations of the philosophy of rugged individualism in an economic system, and might well be called the "ostrich view." Individuals cannot be treated simply as individuals; they are members of groups and share group privileges or disabilities that often conflict with the desires of other groups. It is not clear that the problems of a multiracial society will automatically work themselves out if left alone.

Nor is it clear that America is a melting pot in the sense that group differences are automatically being reduced to a common undifferentiated culture; there is some evidence that nationality groups are tending to blend, though slowly, but that religious groups are coming to be more sharply defined. In certain respects—for example, use of the English language—accommodation to the American scene is progressing; in other respects—as in the tendency toward the formation of class lines—American society is becoming more diversified. As for racial groups, it is likely that the ultimate results of interracial mating, much of which has occurred already, will make it difficult if not impossible to use color as a criterion for social division a few hundred years hence, but the problems of race in America can hardly be allowed to drift for that long.

A second philosophy is built around the idea that citizens should *tolerate differences*. The differences should be recognized for what they are, but the proper attitude is that of "live and let live." Much of the general propaganda about interracial and interreligious relations flows from this kind of thinking.

Tolerance in a world of relativities is doubtless better than intolerance. At best, however, it results in a rather negative approach to group problems; toleration requires no action beyond itself for the improvement of conditions. Further, it makes possible an attitude of condescension, or the dubious assumption that moral neutralism is the proper attitude and that any evaluation of differences is impossible. Most serious of all, this philosophy focuses attention too exclusively on attitudes, ignoring social conditions and patterns that help to create and sustain the attitudes deplored.

A third approach is to seek the *elimination of differences*. That is, all groups should be required, by education or by force, to conform to a common national pattern. When in Rome, one should do as the Romans do. If one does not like that, he is free to go elsewhere. When applied rather mildly, this outlook results in the Americanization programs sponsored by organizations proud of their 100 per cent Americanism. An example of a more strenuous application was given in the Russification policies of the Czars. In its extreme form, this approach leads toward totalitarianism, as in the effort at

Nazification of Germany, with the exile or extinction of groups (most especially the Jews) adjudged to deviate from the national ideal of blood and culture.

While glimpsing clearly the value of unity in a society, advocates of this theory fail to appreciate the value of variety. They seek to universalize their own way of thinking, but are not always willing to share their privileges with the members of marginal groups toward whom their program is directed. They seek not only uniformity, but conformity as well, and coercion of those who will not conform is always a danger. When applied to racial groups, this policy would logically lead to the elimination of characteristics that are not easily eliminated, such as skin color, if the assumption is that the national ideal requires uniformity in this respect. In any event, those who use this approach fail to understand that the creativity and growth of a society depend in part on the presence of variety within its life. A dead level society would soon be a dead society.

A fourth philosophy goes to the other extreme and is based on the *glorification of differences*. Its exponents not only accept cultural differences; they rejoice in them and seek to perpetuate or even to increase them. They are adept at promoting folk dances and sharing exotic foods. They deplore the disappearance of old traditions and customs as the children of immigrants adapt to their new situation.

Doubtless there is much merit in this viewpoint. A

74

society is greatly enriched by having a diversity of customs, just as it is by encouraging a diversity of ideas. But the problem of the cultural pluralists, as the advocates of this approach are most often called, is that of defining the area within which differences shall be encouraged. Should it include access to jobs, so that Negroes will be expected to do a certain type of work? Should it include political behavior, so that Italians would always be expected to vote for the Democratic Party?

Most advocates of cultural pluralism would designate these questions as absurd; they have generally been thinking for the most part about leisure-time activities having to do with "cultural matters" in the narrow sense of that phrase—that is, music, art, diet, religion, and the like. But even these leisure-time activities have some relation to the identification of an individual with a certain group, and the more distinctive they are, the fewer his points of contact with those of other groups. Should Puerto Rican children in the schools of New York City be taught in English or in the language of their parents? The answer will have a considerable bearing on the future economic possibilities of the children.

The problem of a society is always that of striking a balance between unity (not uniformity) and diversity (not anarchy). It must have enough unity to maintain itself and enough diversity to improve itself. There is no static solution to this problem. It is certain that every society errs to some degree at times in one direction or the other, and that its problem then is to redress the balance.

The problem can be restated in terms of the meaning of democracy, as over against totalitarianism (autocracy) on the one hand and anarchy on the other. There have been many approaches to the definition of democracy, in terms of the rights of citizens, or the type of government, or the nature of the political process, or the distribution of wealth and power. Approaches of this kind are rather inconclusive, as the resulting specifications are often found to some extent in countries that are certainly not democratic in character—at least, not in any concept of the term that would be recognized in the traditional democracies of Western Europe and America. For example, the Nazis held periodic elections, and Hitler came to power in the first place through regular parliamentary process. The Communists claim to guarantee a wide range of rights to citizens—a wider range than that to be found in the American Bill of Rights, though there are significant omissions.

The most incisive approach to the definition of democracy lies in examination of the values or moral ideals held to be most precious. They were described most succinctly in the slogan of the French Revolution: "Liberty, Equality, Fraternity." Liberty meant the freedom of each individual to live without undue coercion. Equality meant the recognition of equal worth and opportunity among all individuals. Fraternity was regarded as the social cement that would hold men together: they would guard one another's freedom and strive for equality because they recognized one another as brothers.

When defined in this way, democracy stands in sharp contrast to alternative social systems. Classical capitalism (not exemplified by the capitalism to be found at present in either Europe or America) emphasized the economic freedom and self-interest of the individual and largely ignored equality of opportunity and of the distribution of benefits. Communism destroys liberty in the professed service of equality, though Marxist theory holds that freedom will return in the classless society after all inequality has been destroyed. Nazism simply repudiated both liberty and equality as social ideals: there could be no freedom except in loyalty to the state and allegiance to the Fuhrer, and mankind was to be divided into a Master Race on the one hand and subject and slave peoples on the other.

Democratic theory owes more than is often supposed to ancient Hebrew-Christian teachings. Its central values, liberty and equality, represent modern, secularized variants from basic Christian doctrines. Christianity has affirmed, as had Judaism before it, that man was given freedom by his Creator—a freedom that included even the ability to disobey God himself, as symbolized in the story of the Fall. At the same time, Christianity puts man's freedom within a context of responsibility culminating in the paradox that the truest freedom comes in obedience to Him "whose service is perfect freedom." In Christian perspective freedom is not autonomous and is not to be devoted simply to one's own self-interest; rather it consists in the personal opportunity and responsibility to seek and to do the will of God in relation both to self and to neighbor. Isolated from such foundations, the democratic concept of freedom slips easily into selfishness and anarchy.

The democratic theory of equality is derived from the Christian teachings that God is the Creator of all men and that all are equal in his sight. He cares for and judges all equally. It is intended that men live in community with one another and love their neighbors as themselves, because both self and neighbor are recipients equally of the love of God. Christianity has typically thought of equality in theological and moral terms, rather than slipping into the false assumptions that it is inherent in nature or that it is basically a quantitative concept.

Most important of all, Christianity has grounded liberty and equality in the purposes of God. The eighteenth century philosophers and leaders of the French Revolution substituted Fraternity as the guarantee that these values would be realized. But man's continuing inhumanity to man has become notorious in the twentieth century, and one wonders whether any values that depend for realization merely on a humanistic spirit can inspire loyalty and continue as powerful forces in the ordering of human affairs.

Democracies face a serious problem in that liberty and equality are concepts and values somewhat opposed to each other. If individuals who are not equal by nature in intelligence, cunning, or physical strength are left free to compete on equal terms, they will soon be unequal in power, wealth, and accomplishments. But if an effort is made to restore a rough measure of equality among them, the freedom of certain individuals will inevitably be curbed in the process. How could a nation be conceived in liberty, yet dedicated to the proposition that all men are created equal?

The fact is that a democracy is generally off balance in the realization of its two central ideals. If it allows too much liberty without concern for equality, it drifts toward anarchy, as the United States did in the 1920's. If it emphasizes equality without concern for liberty, it goes toward totalitarianism. Put another way, a democracy must always be busy in remaking itself, in redressing the balance. It can never be a static, fixed society. It can be a planning society, but the plan is never fixed once and for all.

The British symbol is a lion, and the American symbol is an eagle. A better symbol for a democracy would be a duck—on land. A duck walking makes progress by being slightly off balance most of the time without letting the pendulum-motion upset its equilibrium.

If democracy is defined in terms of social ideals, the implication is plain that it can always be accused of hypocrisy. It never quite realizes its ideals; its ethical grasp always exceeds its actual reach. Gunnar Myrdal has centered his study of the Negro American on this problem, which he calls "an American dilemma." The gap between "the American Creed" of freedom and equality on the one hand and the actual practices in American race relations on the other comprises the dilemma.

When applied directly to race relations, democratic theory must choose between the various policies theoretically available. In the last analysis they come down to two, integration and segregation, though many other policies have been proposed on occasion, such as extermination or deportation of the weaker group.

Segregation means the enforced separation of racial groups, either in regard to a few areas of life or in regard to many or all. In view of the biological implications, it nearly always means an effort to separate the groups as far as recognized mating is concerned. It generally includes separating them for educational and economic purposes. The separation may sometimes be undertaken in every aspect of life, as advocated by those who believe in the purest form of *apartheid* in South Africa.

Segregation inevitably involves discriminatory treatment—that is, the limitation of opportunities and achievements for the segregated group. This means limiting the freedom of individuals within that group. Equality is generally denied as one of the first presuppositions of a segregation policy; equality is always denied in the distribution of privileges.

The doctrine that racial groups can be "separate but equal" within the same society has been shown to be a false hope; even in America, with its great wealth, duplicate facilities and opportunities of equal merit have not been achieved. There is not often a genuine and widespread desire on the part of the dominant group to have them really equal; segregation itself, with its element of compulsion, implies the inferiority, and therefore the inferior claims, of the weaker group.

Integration calls for a society in which an individual is free and has equal opportunity to make the most of his life and to participate in the direction of the affairs of the society. He will naturally have certain limitations put on his freedom; absolute freedom for each person would lead to anarchy. But the limitations will not be arbitrary in that they apply to him or his group alone. He may not end with power or privilege exactly equal to that of every other member of the society; exact quantitative equality has not been the democratic social goal. But he will continue to have equality of access to the general privileges of the society—the franchise, jobs, educational opportunities, cultural and religious activities.

Integration has a more positive content than the term desegregation. It implies not merely the elimination of barriers and the removal of compulsory separation. It requires further that people of all racial groups shall join in seeking together to realize the highest ideals of a democracy. It implies responsibility for all as well as opportunity for all, duties as well as rights. It does not necessarily mean that all will be molded into one undifferentiated mass, racially and in other respects; so long as freedom is genuine, there is likely to be diversity within the population. It does mean common commitment to the central goals.

It has sometimes been argued that a middle way between segregation and integration is possible. Sometimes this alternative has been called "bi-racialism," sometimes "parallel development," sometimes "pluralism." The essence of this theory is that separate groups can maintain their separation voluntarily to the mutual advantage of all. Examples most often given are those of various nationality groups living in proximity to others, such as the Scots and British in the British Isles, or the French and British in Canada. It should be noted that in such instances there is no imputation of significant racial differences. There is no clear example on record of the successful maintenance of this middle way over a significant period of time when a strong racial factor was involved or even when it was possible to impute one.

There can be no doubt about the choice a democracy must make as between a policy of segregation and one of integration. The first violates both the central values underlying and inspiring a democracy. The other is aimed at the realization of both as fully as possible.

*Chapter Six*

## THE STRATEGY OF INTEGRATION

There is much debate about the strategy for moving toward an integrated society.

It has been popular to say that education and good will are the best methods for overcoming prejudice. Education can help to remove prejudice insofar as the latter is based on inaccurate information or deficient knowledge. But much prejudice is irrational in character and deep seated in personal needs and fears, and accordingly is little affected by educational approaches. Ideas can be changed, but emotions are rather stubborn.

Of greater importance, the problem of integration is stated wrongly if it is considered to be primarily one of removing prejudice. It is more largely one of removing injustice—that is, of removing the barriers to freedom and equality on the part of segregated groups. Prejudice underlines and reinforces these barriers, and is in turn sustained and recreated in each new generation by them. It is quite clear that most of these barriers can be torn down, and there is evidence that prejudice will decline (though it may be intensified at moments in the process) as the barriers fall.

Education alone has very little effect on the barriers. Indeed, the appeal to education can be used to divert attention from the fundamental task. It can represent a delaying tactic. Thus it used to be said in many circles that the Negro American could never be given the vote or the chance at an excellent job, to say nothing of social equality, until he had achieved education. Even after thousands of Negroes had become well educated, they found themselves still excluded from higher levels of opportunity; the problem now was that the white man had to be educated to accept them. And now that many white men have reached that stage, it will doubtless be argued in some circles that the Negro must now be educated to accept the acceptance.

The cultivation of good will, a favorite theme in the churches, is likewise ambiguous in results. An atmosphere of good will ordinarily provides a better climate in which to seek the solution of difficult problems than does indifference or hatred. But good feeling does not in itself provide the formulas for desegregation and integration. It may actually be used to mask, preserve, and render more bearable a pattern of segregation. It has been claimed that good will, in the sense of solicitude, toward the Negro is greater in the Southern part of the United States than in the remainder of the country, and there is a basis for such a claim. The feeling of concern, however, has itself operated within a framework of paternalism; it has generally been the concern of one who feels superior to one who is deemed inferior and therefore less able to make his own decisions or to look after himself. This kind of good will is spurious when viewed from a larger perspective. But the point is that good will has little content in the first place; it is a matter of the disposition, and the content of the action to follow from it must still be determined.

When one turns from such evasive generalities to more concrete possibilities for strategy, the complexity of the problem becomes appalling. It is not possible to lay down a strategy for the improvement of race relations or the achievement of integration that would be equally valid for all situations, because of the great variety of the situations themselves. For example, legal action has proved to be a very effective device when used on behalf of the Negro in the United States, but it would generally have little or no chance of success if undertaken in support of the Bantu in South Africa.

# The Strategy of Integration

There is no magic formula nor program. But it is possible, on the basis of tested knowledge, to set down certain principles that must underlie any successful strategy. Over a period of several years, a group of social scientists at Cornell University, led by Professor Robin Williams, has studied race relations in various parts of the United States at firsthand, and the following principles, among others, have emerged from their studies: [1]

1. "Sustained interaction between majority and minority is essential."

In fourteen different surveys involving about six thousand persons (North and South; white and Negro; Jewish and Christian), the Cornell scientists found that: "The more contact a person has with other groups, the lower is his level of general prejudice against them." One of the principal characteristics of the situation in South Africa at the present time is the absence of real conversation between leaders of the government and of the Africans. As one African chief complained: "Why cannot they just talk with us? We do not wish to destroy. We need the European friendship and greater knowledge." Nor is there genuinely personal contact across racial lines at any level in South Africa, with rare exceptions. In many communities of the American

[1] *A Manual of Intergroup Relations,* by John P. Dean and Alex Rosen. Chicago, University of Chicago Press, 1955. The principles were worked out with special reference to settlement houses, Y's, and recreational centers, but their implications for other types of situations will be apparent. The phrasing and content of some of the principles and all the comments are my own. Quotations used by permission.

South the degree and friendliness of association between white and Negro have diminished under the new tensions surrounding desegregation of the public schools. If greater difficulties are to be avoided, a community committee, or some such device involving the leadership of both groups, is an essential requirement.

In short, the more we get together under proper conditions, the less prejudiced and more democratic we are likely to be.

2. "Persons inexperienced in intergroup relations frequently alienate minority persons with whom they wish to be friendly by inadvertently expressing themselves in the language of prejudice."

It has been said that a gentleman is "a man who never unintentionally gives offense." The etiquette of good race relations, like all good manners, requires some thought and study in a society whose speech forms and traditions are themselves filled with prejudice. Patronizing attitudes ("I just love Negro music"), weighted phrases ("free, white, and twenty-one"), and epithets ("nigger," "kaffir") can arouse deep resentment.

3. "Intergroup understanding is impeded by ignoring individual and group differences and treating all persons as though they were alike."

It is a most appealing and fair-sounding sentiment to proclaim that one will "treat everybody alike." If this means an effort to be equally fair and understanding toward everybody, the goal is laudable. But the fact is that everybody is not alike emotionally or in terms of cultural traditions. Negroes and Jews in America have often had experiences that have created special sensitivity calling for special understanding, though not for condescension.

4. "An effective intergroup relations program generally requires adequate minority representation among those who develop and guide the activities of the organization."

This does not mean that a Negro or Jew should be on a committee or in Congress simply as a "spokesman for his people." It does mean that agencies concerned for the entire community will avail themselves of the talents to be found in minority groups, and of the inside knowledge that can come only from those who belong to such groups. And it means that representation should be able and active, not merely token in character. The Cornell group listed four criteria for good representation:

"Fullest minority participation in planning policy and program involves the participation of minority persons with insight into minority problems, skills in social relationships with persons of different ethnic and social status, articulateness in discussing minority-majority relations, and the emotional poise to handle touchy subjects and situations without becoming bitter or hostile."

5. "Major changes in individual prejudices occur most quickly and thoroughly from exposure to social

interaction in a new social environment rather than from information and exhortation alone."

Prejudices, having been learned in the first place (at least in the form they take, if not in the tendency toward them), can be unlearned, though the process may often be painful. And it is becoming increasingly clear that the best teacher of unlearning is a congenial situation in which the prejudiced person can become acquainted with actual persons who belong to the group he had disparaged.

It is doubtful that prejudice has been reduced very much by campaigns of propaganda against it, through posters, television programs, and the like. It appears to have been affected to somewhat larger degree by lectures and sermons stressing tolerance, and by group discussions. It is most effectively dispelled when personal experience is broadened to include pleasant relationships with a great many people from the group formerly despised.

6. "Within wide limits, prejudiced persons will accept and participate in a thoroughly mixed and integrated setting if integrated patterns are established and accepted as appropriate by other participants in that situation."

They may not like it, but most people tend voluntarily when in Rome to do as the Romans do. Even many of those who are prejudiced will conform to local customs. If the customs themselves are changed—for example, if railroads actually adopt a policy of serving meals without discrimination—many persons who resent the change will nevertheless continue to go to the diner. And there is evidence that the resentment itself will often diminish or disappear in time.

In short, it is not necessary, as is often supposed, to get rid of prejudice before overcoming racial discrimination in this practice or in that. If the pattern of discrimination on which prejudice feeds is itself changed, the prejudice may wither. In such matters one may work from either end, or both.

From studies made in twenty American communities, the Cornell scholars concluded that "segregation and discrimination are not closely related to the intensity of prejudice in the individual." They further concluded that the amount of prejudice a person has may have little to do with his behavior if he is placed in a non-segregated situation. Studies of integration in housing, hospitals, the Armed Services, and elsewhere have shown that many whites who objected vigorously in advance or at the outset of desegregation have quickly come to accept the new situation and to live within it. Whatever happened to their prejudice, their behavior changed.

But how are patterns of discrimination or segregation to be changed if they are supported by a prejudiced public opinion? It is obvious that change will be difficult if not impossible as long as public opinion is sufficiently uniform and vigorous. But nearly every community has a great deal of inconsistency within its own practices, and there are always plastic points at which changes can be introduced; there may be little objection to mixed trade unions, or even mixed churches, in a setting in which the issue of a nonsegregated swimming pool would be explosive.

Further, decisions about the practices of particular institutions in a community are seldom really made by "public opinion," though appeal to that vague force may rationalize refusal to make decisions differently. Decisions are seldom made directly by "the rank-and-file"; most often they are made by those entrusted with policy making. In a democratic situation there is always an ultimate appeal to the total constituency. But the constituency itself expects leadership. And the leadership often has far more latitude, even in ticklish matters of race, than it supposes, as the variety of patterns to be found in almost any community will attest. Those who are actually in a position to make changes of policy within a certain organization or situation have, therefore, a great opportunity and grave responsibility to demonstrate leadership. A genuinely interracial, nonsegregated situation seldom "just grows"; it must be planned.

In making plans for policy change, the Cornell study advises, several particular points may be kept in mind:

a. It is generally better to begin with moral principles, such as the American Creed of equality, rather than bogging down at the beginning in concrete problems.

b. It is better to have a positive policy than no policy, in order that the position may be perfectly clear to all.

c. In case the organization is an affiliate of a national body, the expressed policy of the national body can often be very useful in the local situation.

d. Examples of successful integration in kindred or neighboring institutions can often be very helpful and reassuring.

e. No effort should be made to stifle potential opposition by facing it with an accomplished fact, especially if the potential danger lies in the group responsible for making policy. But it is well to study in advance the possibility of opposition and the capability for meeting it.

f. Even if no policy of desegregation is possible at the moment, a policy adopting desegregation as a goal to be achieved as rapidly as possible provides a direction for future movement.

7. "Desegregation that proceeds by firm and decisive steps backed by the responsible authorities is more readily accepted and taken for granted than a halting desegregation that appears unsure of itself."

When, by Federal Court order, twelve Negro pupils were admitted to the high school of Clinton, Tennessee, (population 3,712) it became necessary for more than six hundred Tennessee National Guardsmen to be sent into the town to keep order. After several days of agitation, abetted by outsiders who had come to preach pro-segregation, mobs had formed in the streets and law and order had broken down. The Governor promptly sent in state policemen and then the National Guard. This example of prompt and decisive action by responsible authorities will doubtless give pause to those in other situations of potential violence. There is no substitute for firm action in any area of social controversy.

8. "Successful efforts to eliminate segregation or discrimination usually have two phases: (1) getting fairplay policies established and (2) working to bring about compliance with and enforcement of these policies."

It is often possible to change the policies and practices of a community without going to the legislature or the town council or the courts. Committees on race relations, councils for unity, and other such groups designed for survey of the situation and action to improve it have often been highly effective. Sometimes they have been official, under appointment by the mayor or governor or president. At other times they have been entirely unofficial, organized and directed by community leaders who have become convinced that this explosive area of a community's life must not be left to chance.

In some places, notably in the Union of South Africa,

it is unrealistic to suppose that the authority of government can be used toward a goal of integration. To the contrary, the power of the government itself is being used in precisely the opposite direction, as it was in the American South at the turn of this century.

It has been demonstrated in certain other places, particularly in the United States, that strong governmental action, whether through legislation or court decisions or executive orders, can be highly effective in changing the pattern of race relations. It is often argued that you cannot legislate away prejudice, which is a matter of the human heart beyond the reach of the police. There is doubtless some truth to this statement when it is applied to a living individual. But it is possible by legislation or other official act to change conditions that perpetuate prejudice from generation to generation. Of equal importance, it is possible to prevent actions and to overcome disabilities by which minority groups are disadvantaged and oppressed. Action can be controlled by law, though never perfectly, and new doors of opportunity can be opened.

Thus by a series of presidential edicts segregation in the armed forces of the United States has been overcome. So has discrimination with regard to jobs under government contracts and in Federal employment. More than a dozen states have passed statutes having to do with fair employment practices, and the results have been even better than anticipated, with persuasion being the usual procedure rather than resort to judicial determination. Comparable statutes and commissions to deal with fair educational practices have encountered more subtle difficulties but have made progress. Some states and municipalities have adopted statutes against segregation in public housing or housing given tax advantages.

Most of the provinces in Canada now have legislation, largely passed during the last five years, to insure fairness in employment practices and in access to such public accommodations as restaurants. There is also a national anti-discrimination law that covers railways and ships.

States in the South have likewise indicated their belief that legislation is an effective method for control of race relations. They established a pattern of segregation in the first place very largely through use of state laws. More recently, the majority of Southern states (all but four) have repealed the poll tax laws (which most had adopted about fifty years ago as an instrument to control voting). South Carolina has passed an anti-lynching law, after a great many efforts to obtain a Federal law of this kind had failed. Since the Supreme Court's decision in 1954 that segregation in the public schools is unconstitutional, a number of states have resorted to legislation in an effort to thwart implementation of the Court's ruling. Legislation can be used to implement either side of a public issue; as in the case of all legislative enactments, its effectiveness will depend on the vigor of enforcement.

A group of social psychologists had studied scores of successful attempts at desegregation before the Supreme Court handed down its decision. The group reached the following general conclusion: [1]

The accomplishment of efficient desegregation with a minimum of social disturbance depends upon:

A. A clear and unequivocal statement of policy by leaders with prestige and other authorities;

B. Firm enforcement of the changed policy by authorities and persistence in the execution of this policy in the face of initial resistance;

C. A willingness to deal with violations, attempted violations, and incitement to violations by resort to the law and strong enforcement action;

D. A refusal of the authorities to resort to, engage in, or tolerate subterfuges, gerrymandering or other devices for evading the principles and the fact of desegregation;

E. An appeal to the individuals concerned in terms of their religious principles of brotherhood and their acceptance of the American traditions of fair play and equal justice.

Comparison of these successful instances of desegregation also revealed that the amount of time involved in the process was not clearly related to the end result. In some instances there was a protracted educational period in order to "prepare" the people affected; in others there was immediate desegregation once the is-

[1] "Desegregation: An Appraisal of the Evidence," by Kenneth B. Clark, in *The Journal of Social Issues,* Vol. IX, No. 4 (1953), p. 54.

sue had been raised. It was clear, however, that all the units of a certain type of facility in a community—for example, playgrounds—should be desegregated at the same time if the most effective results are to be achieved; otherwise, there is confusion and the desegregated units from which the whites have retreated tend to be taken over wholly by minority groups, really preserving the pattern of segregation.

There can be little doubt that a program of integration, when defined in law or policy statement and enforced with reasonable vigor, can be successful even in a rather hostile setting. A test of this question is currently under way in certain Southern states in America, where efforts of various kinds are being made to evade the decision of the Supreme Court outlawing segregation in the public schools. The dilemma of these states is real to them, and deserves sympathy from the remainder of the nation, which itself has been slow to move on such matters until required to do so. It must be admitted that very little progress toward integration is likely to occur in certain Southern communities in the immediate future, because of the great difficulties involved.

The Southern apprehension is shared by white and Negro alike—though nearly every shade of opinion is to be found within the South. Many white parents feel that it is unfair that their children should pay the deficit in Negro education accumulated over the last hundred years; that is, they fear that the educational level in the middle grades will necessarily be lowered because of the inferior training thus far of Negro pupils who would be integrated. Such a problem is a real one, though wise educational administration can do much to mitigate it. But the parents who advance this argument might well remember that they themselves were probably involved in the perpetuation of a "separate and unequal" system of public education, and that in any case their argument loses most of its force when applied to integration in the first grade or at the level of the graduate school.

Many Negro parents are also apprehensive about integration; though there is much evidence that most support it in principle and emotionally, they know that serious problems can be created for the first generation of "integrating Negroes": the danger of violence or constant insult, the hazards arising from a sudden increase in the extent and vigor of competition, the possibility of boycotts and other forms of pressure against the Negro community. From one perspective, race relations have worsened greatly in several Southern states since the edict of the Supreme Court with regard to de-segregation of the public schools: flaming crosses have appeared in places, the growing tendency to elect Negroes to public office has been reversed, a few hundred Negro teachers have lost their jobs (though several times as many are now teaching united classes), and the general relations between the races have suffered from a renewal of avoidance and suspicion.

Any period of transition is likely to have its special costs to the groups involved. But the Southern states that have refused to comply honestly with the Supreme Court's decision are in an untenable dilemma. They can hardly resort to force or secede again from the Union; any such course is unthinkable and would be utterly disastrous. They can pretend to give up their public schools, but any such devious course is likely to lead to further trouble with the Supreme Court and ultimately with their own citizenry; several of the laws passed toward that end have been so vague and confused as to suggest near-hysteria rather than a well-conceived plan. The inescapable fact, North and South, is that desegregation in various facilities, including the public schools, is the law of the land, and ultimately that law is bound to prevail if the nation is to avoid anarchy and loss of self-respect. A few states cannot for long either deceive or thwart the great majority. The Supreme Court might conceivably change its mind, of course, but that seems to be most unlikely.

Furthermore, developments outside the legal and judicial field are sure to exert powerful pressure toward desegregation. The traditional pattern of race relations in the Southern states had been considerably undermined, even before the Supreme Court became very active in this field, by the industrialization and urbanization of many parts of the South. Further development along these lines is likely to be hindered seriously by the deterioration of the system of public education, and even more by the possibilities of racial violence. By and large, economic pressures are on the side of integration; while racial feeling may override them at times, in the long run people may be as much concerned to eat as to discriminate.

The power of the Negro community in America as a whole is also a factor making for integration throughout the country. Between 1890 and 1950, the percentage of the Negro population living in the South declined from 90 per cent to 68 per cent. Between 1940 and 1950, the South lost more than a million Negroes by migration to other parts of the country; while the total gain in Negro population in that region during the decade was still 150,000, the gain in the remainder of the country was about two million.

These millions of Negroes living in other parts of the nation have often come to have a considerable amount of influence in their communities and, in the aggregate, in the nation. Their pressure toward integration is certain to be continuous and influential.

Their principal organizational vehicles are such agencies as the National Association for the Advancement of Colored People (to which many whites belong), the National Urban League, and many other such agencies. Hundreds of organizations dealing with problems of integration are now in existence in the nation, at all levels from that of the local community up to the national scene. Whatever segments of the white population may think about them, many of these organizations have proved that they can be extremely effective; the sincerity of their purposes and the legitimacy of their methods are seldom called into question by objective observers. Some have emphasized a legal approach (*e.g.,* the NAACP); others have sought better economic opportunities for members of minority groups (*e.g.,* the National Urban League); still others have focused on better housing or educational opportunities or community contacts. All told, they represent a body of public opinion and influence that is certain to prevail in national policy, especially in view of the fact that they have basic American traditions of equality and freedom for all on their side.

Whatever may be done by government, organized groups, or impersonal social forces, individuals still have a responsibility for the management of their own attitudes and conduct. Opportunities for personal participation in the movement toward better race relations vary greatly, of course, but there must be few persons who cannot find some way to contribute. Most of the larger Protestant denominations and the other human relations agencies have published handbooks containing suggestions for action by individuals and by church groups. One may be depressed at the magnitude of the problems remaining before a great many American communities and states, but it is always possible to find ways in which to make one's own contribution, large or small. The place to begin is in one's own personal relationships and in the circles, especially the voluntary groups, in which one moves.

*Chapter Seven*

# THE INVOLVEMENT OF THE LOCAL CHURCHES

Voluntary groups—that is, groups composed of those who vote on new members or who elect to join—bid fair to be the last strongholds of segregation in America and in other parts of the world. Being private in character they are less subject to public opinion or to regulation by law than are such public facilities as schools or transportation systems. Further, a cardinal principle in their purpose is that of congeniality; they are the enclaves in which birds of a feather flock together.

Among voluntary groups the churches are most conspicuous of all, both in their extent and size and also in their racial composition. It has been said that "eleven o'clock on Sunday morning is the most segregated hour in the week." One could qualify that conclusion: eleven o'clock on Saturday night is even more segregated for the country club set, and other purely social clubs are in general more completely uni-racial than are the churches.

Its record indicates clearly, however, that the church is the most segregated major institution in American society. It has lagged behind the Supreme Court as the conscience of the nation on questions of race, and it has fallen far behind trade unions, factories, schools, department stores, athletic gatherings, and most other major areas of human association as far as the achievement of integration in its own life is concerned.

Statistics can tell the story to some degree, though church statistics are sometimes compiled without systematic planning and are not completely reliable. For purposes of illustration, and because the Negro American comprises the largest segregated group in the churches, the analysis may be confined for the moment to the Negro and his relation to the churches. Furthermore, it is now possible to portray statistically the recent changes in the pattern of Negro church membership.

Using figures drawn mostly from 1943-44, Dr. Frank Loescher estimated a decade ago that 8,300,000 of the fourteen million Negroes in the United States belonged to some church.[1] He concluded that approximately eight million were Protestants, the remainder (300,-000) Roman Catholics. Of the Protestants, seven and a half million were in separate Negro denominations, and only half a million were in predominantly "white" denominations, with the Methodist Church having 60 per cent of the latter group and setting them apart in a separate jurisdiction.[2] Thus nearly all Negro Protestants were in their own organizations, having little contact with white Christians as such except in occasional ministerial associations or special meetings and in such interdenominational bodies as the Federal Council of Churches.[3]

Even those Negroes who belonged to predominantly white denominations were largely segregated at the level of the local congregation, though their representatives might have some contact with white Christians in synods or state conferences (seldom in the South) and generally did at the level of their national bodies. Loescher sent inquiries to all the local churches (17,900 in number) affiliated with six major white denominations: from a total of 6,356 replies it was learned that

---

[1] *The Protestant Church and the Negro,* by Frank S. Loescher, pp. 51-52. New York, Association Press, 1948.

[2] For a careful and objective study of the complicated arrangement in the Methodist Church, see *Negro Segregation in the Methodist Church,* by Dwight W. Culver. New Haven, Yale University Press, 1953.

[3] One of the eight agencies that later merged to form the National Council of the Churches of Christ in the United States of America.

860 churches had members from more than one racial group. When a more detailed questionnaire was sent to these churches, 389 replies were received, revealing that 290 of them were white churches with Negro participants, most of them in New York State and New England. The number of Negroes involved was very small: 1,132 attended church occasionally but were not members, and 1,320 were members. Other local churches reported participation of Japanese Americans, Mexicans, and other groups in white churches.

Though incomplete, these statistics indicate that less than 2 per cent of the white congregations had Negro members at the end of World War II and that probably considerably less than one per cent of the Negroes in American Protestantism were included in white congregations. The mixture of racial groups in a congregation, where it occurred, hardly deserved that description in most instances; typically it involved the membership of two to four Negroes in an overwhelmingly "white" church, generally in a rural area or small town with a Negro community too small to be of public importance or to form, or be segregated into, a church of its own. There were very few genuinely interracial churches even in the cities with shifting populations and mixed neighborhoods.

In short, the segregation of Negroes into separate churches was practically universal throughout the United States a decade ago. There was very little difference between Southern and non-Southern churches in this regard. Nor was there very much difference between Southern denominations and Northern or national ones in the way in which they organized their presbyteries and other intermediate bodies into segregated units *in the South;* denominations, with only one or two exceptions, adopted the regional pattern for their organizational structure. This was true even for denominations that had been in the forefront of the abolitionist crusade a century earlier.

The size or geographical extent of a denomination, the liturgical or informal mode of its worship, the centralized or congregational form of ecclesiastical polity, the type of theology prevailing—none of these factors appears to have had any special relevance to segregation in the churches. Though these factors varied, segregation was well-nigh universal. The Protestant Episcopal Church and the Congregational Christian Churches appeared to have slightly more mixed churches than other denominations; a survey in 1945 revealed that about 6 per cent of the Congregational churches included some degree of racial mixture. Some of the smaller groups—notably the Primitive Baptists, the Quakers, and Jehovah's Witnesses—were, and are, substantially more interracial in practice than the larger denominations, but other small sects have been extremely nativist and anti-Negro.

The over-all statistical picture of segregation in the

churches has not changed very much in the last ten years. The size of the entire Negro community in America has grown to about sixteen million. Figures pertaining usually to the year 1955 show a total membership in Negro denominations of 10,043,552, with 95 per cent of this total accounted for by the five largest bodies.[1] A reasonably reliable estimate would put the number of Negro members of predominantly white denominations at slightly more than 600,000, with about 375,000 in the Methodist Church alone. It is still true, as in 1945, that 94 per cent of the Negro Protestants are in Negro denominations, having few religious relationships with other Protestants.

The most significant changes in the last ten years have taken place at that level of church life often supposed to be most unchangeable with regard to racial matters, namely, the local congregation. A study of three denominations—the United Lutheran Church in America, the Congregational Christian Churches, and the Presbyterian Church in the U.S.A.—all of which had been included in Loescher's earlier survey—was carried out between 1950 and 1954.[2] Questionnaires were

[1] Compiled from *Yearbook of American Churches,* edited by Benson Y. Landis, 1957 edition. New York, National Council of Churches, 1956. The five denominations are: the National Baptist Convention, U.S.A., Inc.; the National Baptist Convention of America; the African Methodist Episcopal Church; the African Methodist Episcopal Zion Church; the Colored Methodist Episcopal Church.

[2] The study was made under the sponsorship of the Department of Racial and Cultural Relations, National Council of Churches. Its re-

mailed to the 13,597 local churches in the three denominations, and 4,810 replied. Of this number, 1,331 reported racial mixture in membership or in some activity of the church, with the former more frequent. Thus about 28 per cent of the churches replying could report some kind of interracial character, or 10 per cent of the total number of churches involved. It is probable that the churches from whom no reply was received were silent in most cases because they had nothing to report. And the minority group present in mixed churches constituted more than 10 per cent of the church membership in less than one per cent of the churches. Even so, the change in the churches as contrasted with the picture of ten years earlier is very significant. Of the racially mixed churches, 110 were in the Southeast, with Negroes involved in forty-five instances.

A more intensive study was then made of 405 of the mixed churches. Minority participants in these churches were found to comprise 2.7 per cent of the total membership, with the range by denominations varying from one per cent to 7 per cent. Acceptance of their membership as a normal event had been the case in a majority of the churches, prolonged educational preparation of the membership to receive them had oc-

sults are summarized in "Racial Integration in Three Protestant Denominations," by Alfred Kramer, in *The Journal of Educational Sociology,* October, 1954 pp. 59-68.

curred rather seldom, and official policy discussions had taken place in only a small percentage of cases. Perhaps for this very reason—that is, the refusal to expand the question of admission into a "big issue," thereby causing fears to rise and tempers to mount— it was reported that only twenty-six of the 237,476 members of the churches had severed their connection because members of minority groups were brought in, or one in nine thousand. In contrast to this minimum loss of support, every appraisal reported that the net effect of the departure of the disgruntled member was beneficial to the church in spiritual insight, fellowship, and human assets for the church.

As far as could be ascertained, the initial contact between the church and the future participant from a minority group was made by a representative of the church in only one fourth of the instances. And it became clear that *local* church policy and *local* leadership were important factors in acceptance of the new participants; denominational pronouncements were adjudged to have been of little value, perhaps because most church members knew little or nothing about them.

Other recent surveys support the conclusion that racial mixture in local congregations is increasing significantly. Response to a questionnaire in 1956 from 182 Unitarian churches revealed that nearly 40 per cent of them had Negro members, as compared with 31 per cent in a survey two years earlier. The Disciples of Christ also reported in 1956 on a similar survey: of 2,051 congregations that had replied to an inquiry, 464—scattered through forty states—were racially mixed to some degree, including twenty-one congregations in the South. Members of minority racial groups were found in these Disciples' congregations in significant numbers; all told, the membership of churches reporting two or more races in their congregations included 631 Negroes, 753 Japanese Americans, 433 Indians, 754 Chinese Americans, and 237 Chinese nationals.

The presence of a few members of a minority group in a church circle does not mean that integration, in the sense of full inclusion in the life and work of the church, has taken place. It may mean only that desegregation has begun. Church membership alone can be a formal affair. But it is rather surprising that the local church, often deemed to be the last preserve of segregation, has begun to change its ways so rapidly in the last ten years.[1]

It should be noted that the movement toward integration in the last few years has taken place chiefly in existing churches, rather than through the creation of new ones. Earlier in the 1940's, a number of new inter-

[1] For many examples of this development in local churches, see *Progress Against Prejudice*, by Robert W. Root. New York, Friendship Press, 1957.

racial churches were deliberately established in certain cities, in an effort to provide religious association across racial lines and to set an example for the existing churches. Doubtless these efforts did help to break the wall of segregation. But they were often rather artificial in composition, unrelated to a given neighborhood or tradition. While they served as a training ground for leadership, they also had a tendency to concentrate the leaders in interracial matters in a single place. Most serious of all, the principle of racial inclusiveness was hardly the proper basis on which to establish a church in the first place, though the indifference of most churches in this respect offered adequate provocation. But the problem all the time was not that of building a few symbolic interracial churches; it was rather that of opening the doors of all churches to sincere believers, without reference to nationality or color. Movement in this latter direction has now gained notable momentum.

The fact remains that segregation is still overwhelmingly the pattern that prevails in local churches. Very few, if any, churches have a legal or formal policy to require it; Negroes generally assume that they would not be welcome in most white churches, and whites generally take it for granted that Negroes will stay away. The present situation is a result of historical and social developments, reinforced by continuing fear and prejudice. Though a few separate Negro churches were organized before the Civil War, it was customary in the ante-bellum South for slaves to attend church with the white people and to sit in a gallery or other segregated section. In many places the slaves were forbidden to hold separate religious services, lest such services become breeding places for revolts. After the war, the emancipated Negroes were either forced out of the white churches or, as was more often the case, invited to remain under the previous arrangements. A few accepted that kind of status; many white Methodist churches in the South had Negro members until late in the 1870's, often in some numbers, and comparable examples could be found in other denominations. But the vast majority of the Negroes preferred to have churches of their own and to manage their own affairs, rather than be discriminated against inside the church. Besides, they could hardly forget that most white churches in the South had supported slavery. The great rise of Negro churches and denominations took place accordingly in the decade following the close of the war.

Segregation has prevailed to the present time for many reasons. The rise of prejudice on the part of white church members, associated with fears (largely unwarranted) that admission of non-whites would cause loss of members and support, led to practices that made the Negro and other minority groups feel unwelcome in a white church. White ministers seldom called on non-white families or invited them to church; recruitment of members has followed racial lines. If a Negro presented himself for seating in a white church, he might be turned away or else segregated from the white congregation. It is not true that "Negroes prefer their own churches" in the sense in which white people generally use that statement; there is overwhelming evidence that most Negroes oppose segregation as enforced exclusion. But nearly all prefer their own churches to inferior status in white congregations.

The Negro church quickly came to occupy a unique and central place in its community. It was the first, and for decades almost the only, organization entirely under the control of Negroes. As such it came to be the major channel for expression of their views and emotions, for the achievement of status and the development of leadership. Its ministers could speak to the new condition of their parishioners more precisely than could any white minister; however well-intentioned the latter might be, he had not shared the experience of slavery and emancipation. The Negro church came to be more closely related to the daily life of its members than the white church could hope to be—to their politics, economic problems, recreation, and aspirations. In relations with the white community it has been for the most part a defensive and accommodating institution, but it has often modified the harshness of caste and been the birthplace of schools, social organizations, and other facilities that have improved the condition of the Negro community as a whole.

The special services of the Negro church to its constituents should not obscure the fact that its theology, rituals, forms of organization, and the like are very similar to those of the white churches, and often identical. Nor should it be assumed that the Negro church is a *segregating* institution, any more than it should be assumed that every white church without Negro members deliberately practices segregation. Although the very existence of the Negro church reinforces the caste system and establishes certain vested interests in the maintenance of the status quo, that is not its intention. Almost without exception it would welcome non-Negro worshipers to its services and to membership; sometimes, especially in the South, its welcome is too cordial, with visitors being taken to the front rows and frequently called on "to say a few words." But there can be no doubt of its open-door policy; some years ago eight hundred Negro churches were asked if they objected to attendance by white persons and not one replied in the affirmative. Actually there are comparatively few white members of predominantly Negro congregations even in the North and West; while the question has not been studied, the percentage is probably smaller than that of Negroes in predominantly white congregations.

It is not true that most Negro Protestant leaders de-

sire the continuation of segregation in the churches,
lest they lose their privileged status in the Negro community and find it more difficult to compete with whites
for ecclesiastical posts. A dozen years ago more than a
hundred of them joined in a statement to white churchmen in which they asserted:

Freedom of worship, if it means anything, means freedom to worship God across racial lines and freedom for
a man or woman to join the church of his or her choice,
irrespective of race. Segregated churches fall short of the
requirements of the Christian ideal. . . . When the
church presents the open door, we may still have what
we call Negro and white churches, and they may be
separate churches, but not racially segregated churches.

Probably there would be no cataclysmic change in
church membership or attendance if every Christian
church announced that it was open to all sincere worshipers without regard to race. There has been enough
experience in racially mixed churches in recent years
to show that willingness to "accept" non-whites in white
churches is not likely alone to produce much change,
just as the traditional open-door attitude of Negro
churches has failed to bring in many white members.
But the regard for the churches would change profoundly in the minds of members of minority groups
and of observers in other parts of the world—and in the
minds of white churchmen themselves. Genuine integration requires much more, however, than a statement
of policy, important as that is. It requires the authentic

incorporation of minorities into the life and leadership of the churches.

The conditions that produced the Negro church are not yet outmoded. But its future is being called seriously into question, as is that of Negro schools and colleges, at a time when desegregation is proceeding rapidly in other areas of society. It is no longer the only significant institution in the Negro community, and such agencies as the Negro press and the NAACP have largely taken over the leadership once exercised, often rather haltingly, by the church. More indirectly, its influence is felt through the many local spokesmen for the NAACP who are also religious leaders. The prestige of the Negro ministry, which was formerly *the* profession open to young men, has declined rapidly, perhaps because its educational level has remained low, and recruitment for the profession has come to be a major problem.

Innumerable divisions in the church create confusion to rival that of the white churches; there are about twenty-five denominations and uncounted smaller sects and coteries, organized in many instances around a single leader and often meeting in store fronts or residences. The average congregation is much smaller than in white churches and much less capable of supporting an adequate program or ministry; most urban centers have two or three times as many churches as are needed. Most serious of all, Negro churches are reported to be losing their young people faster than white churches, and they are likely to lose them faster still as these young people find themselves more largely integrated in other aspects of American life but still segregated in the churches. Add to all these difficulties the problem the church has faced in trying to follow the vast migration of Negroes in recent years and to adapt to impersonal, overcrowded urban conditions of life, and the prospects for the Negro church are seen to be rather uncertain.

The pattern of segregation in the churches continues to be reinforced, however, by other factors. The most important of these is residential segregation. Through one device or another most minority groups are still concentrated in particular areas of a city, especially in the inner city area surrounding the central business section. This area was formerly inhabited for the most part in many cities by immigrant groups, who were largely Roman Catholic in affiliation and who have moved in large numbers to the suburbs as their economic situation improved. The inner city has now been taken over in a number of places by Negroes, whose Southern religious background makes them overwhelmingly Protestant in religious preferences. Wherever it may be located, there is generally a "Negro section," North or South.

Residential concentration of minority groups helps to explain the continuation of segregated churches. A survey of seventy-six churches in polyglot Detroit some years ago evoked from more than half of them the response that no Negroes were resident in their neighborhoods, and three fourths replied that there were no churches of Negroes or other minority groups in the vicinity. As a consequence of such racial isolation, most churches appear to have very little consciousness of a race question in their own affairs or in those of their community, except when a riot or other episode disturbs their serenity. A great many ministers and others who are sincerely troubled by the organization of the church along racial lines are rather perplexed as to an alternative, until such time as residential barriers are removed.

Churches located in so-called "transitional zones," where a new group (often Negro) is moving in and the old settlers are moving out, have special opportunities to transcend race in their composition. For many years, the usual procedure was that of selling a church building formerly occupied by the retreating whites to a Negro congregation. Loescher found no instance ten years ago of a church in a transitional zone that had a preponderance of white members but also admitted Negroes. The situation has changed markedly in the last decade: a great many white churches have refused to follow their members to the suburbs, choosing instead to remain where they were and attempt to minister to their new type of community. A large percentage of the mixed churches is to be found in situations of that kind. The old "downtown churches" may find a new source of constituents also among the newcomers.

The influence of boards of home missions has often been decisive in helping a church in an inner city or transitional zone to stand its ground and to minister effectively to the new residents of its area, instead of yielding to the temptation to sell the church building to Negroes and relocate. Many churches still follow the old pattern, but in a rapidly increasing number of instances, mission grants and advice from home mission boards have encouraged declining churches to adapt their programs and replenish their constituencies from the new occupants of their changing neighborhoods. A great many mixed churches have resulted, especially in the larger cities.

Economic factors also influence racial segregation in the churches. As Myrdal and other observers have pointed out, many Negro churches are very much like certain white churches of lower income groups in important respects, such as equipment, type of service, tendencies to emotionalism, a less-educated ministry, and the like. The official boards of Negro churches are often made up of minor supervisors, janitors, clerks, cooks, and other persons of low income and limited opportunity. On the other hand, the corresponding white churches have frequently been more jealous of their racial purity than have more affluent congregations. The churches have had little success in bridging the gulf between social classes, especially in the cities; most congregations are composed predominantly of people from the same general level. When this problem is added to that of racial stratification, the difficulties of integration are compounded. It may be that the churches will not be able to overcome racial segregation significantly in their lives until they learn also to break down class lines.

The most serious factor helping to preserve segregation in the churches is a deficiency on the part of the churches themselves—a deficiency in their understanding of the true nature and purpose of the church. To use Biblical terms, the church is the body of Christ, the new people of God, a redeemed Israel. Social distinctions of whatever kind have no place in this new community; as will be seen, there is no Biblical basis for them and very little basis in twenty centuries of Christian experience. All true believers are equal before the altar and at the communion table. All are equal before God.

The churches in America and in some other countries affirm all these things easily enough, but they do not seem really to understand the implications. The more common view of the local church seems to be that it is some kind of social club. It may be that the Protestant Reformation, with its emphasis on the individual, helped to obscure the concept of the church as a community, though the doctrine of the priesthood of all believers should help to offset that loss. In any event, congeniality appears to be valued more in a congregation than common fidelity to a single Lord. This appears to be more largely true in Protestant churches than in Roman Catholic ones; the centrality and objectivity of the Mass elevate worshipers to a common plane, and Catholic churches seem to have fewer marginal social events than Protestants do. In many Protestant parishes the semi-social functions require more time from members than the worship services. Under these circumstances there is a great temptation to use such social criteria as race or class as standards of acceptability for membership.

A typical formula for excluding Negroes from membership in white churches was worked out by an American bishop. He said that the church, as a divine institution, must hold that all men are equal under God. As a social institution, however, it must reject interracial churches lest they become an opening wedge to social equality. The logic in this formula is comparable to that of a clergyman who told his congregation that the church and the CIO could have nothing to do with each other because the former is interested in eternal salvation and the latter in material benefits in this world; a member of the congregation decided, with perspicacity, to commit his material needs to the care of the CIO and his spiritual needs to the church.

Efforts are frequently made to use the church as a means toward some other end. Politicians, labor leaders, spokesmen for racial groups—a good many people with a special purpose in mind—woo the favor of the church. The church is not properly used for some extrinsic achievement. But at present it actually is used in the United States to support segregation; it is so used by its members, through the continuation of their racial congregations. The church is required only to be truly the church, true to its own essential nature and purpose. When this comes to pass, segregation in its life will be abolished.

There is no one formula by which these buttresses to segregation in the local church can be overcome. Preaching that looks toward eventual integration may prepare the way, or it may solidify opposition. Provision for interracial gatherings that would include both religious and social dimensions would begin to "break the ice." Many churches have started with interracial vacation Bible schools or Sunday schools, or with a Negro teacher in the church school. Young people's groups have often been more adventurous than their elders in making contacts and exchanging visits across racial lines; women's groups have been more willing than official boards. A staff member (not in a menial role) from another racial group can help, if able and personable, to break down stereotypes. Study groups, institutes, and other special educational devices may be useful.

Ultimately a church needs to declare its policy if it expects to achieve integration, and then persist in it even if objection is raised. It may do this in the form of a statement on its bulletin board or in its calendar—not to the effect that it is an interracial church, because it is not the business of the church to be either racial or interracial, but through the assurance that all sincere worshipers will be welcome. Or it may instruct its pastor quietly to recruit members from other racial groups. Or it may begin negotiations to merge with a neighboring church of different racial composition, though such mergers are often tedious and delicate operations.

Once members of minority groups have been brought in, it is very important that they have more than an official or token relationship to the church. They need to be incorporated fully into the program and fellowship of the body if the reception of them is to be more than a gesture. And the new type of relationships within the church will need to be carried over into relationships in other areas of life. It may be easier to worship together than to go to a church supper together, and easier to do the latter than to demonstrate that the bonds of faith still hold outside the church where the world is watching.

*Chapter Eight*

# RACE RELATIONS ELSEWHERE IN
# THE CHURCH

American Protestantism has at the present time no master strategy for the achievement of integration. It is not clear whether the movement should proceed primarily at the level of the local church or through the merger of denominations or through inter-denominational ventures. Nor is it clear as to whether minority churches are to be assimilated to white ones, or the reverse, or a two-way process is to be followed. Certainly no one procedure will prevail in all instances.

Denominational divisions among the churches, white and non-white, not only render the formulation of a master plan difficult; they also hinder integration in many other ways. Denominations have varying degrees of control over local churches, and they are generally skeptical about the loss of churches through mergers or the loss of members to other churches. Institutional interests, as viewed in the short run, are most often in favor of the status quo. Progress toward integration on the national level depends in part on the progress of the ecumenical movement, the movement toward church unity. This is true also in the local community, where a local council of churches, if genuinely inclusive of the churches in the community and really vested with the authority and means to exercise leadership, can do a great deal more toward removal of racial barriers in the churches and in the society than can individual churches or denominational ventures.

Significant changes in race relations have taken place in areas of church life other than the local church in the last decade. Nearly all national church gatherings, whether denominational or interdenominational in character, now try to make certain that segregation will not be encountered by any delegates. In 1950, the segregation of Negro commissioners at the General Assembly of the Presbyterian Church in the U. S. was abolished. The Presiding Bishop of the Protestant Episcopal Church dramatically moved the meeting of the General Convention in 1955 from Houston, Texas, to Honolulu because guarantees could not be given that segregation or discrimination would not be encountered by Negro delegates in Houston. When a Negro delegate to the General Council of the Congregational Christian Churches, meeting in Omaha in 1956, was refused admission to an American Legion clubhouse that had advertised rooms for rent, the Council authorized its Executive Committee to take proper steps to assist the aggrieved delegate, with legal action being suggested as one possible alternative.

Notable changes have taken place also at intermediate levels of ecclesiastical organization, such as synods and state conferences. The Presbyterian Church in the U.S. has abolished its separate synod for Negro members; in that step the Southern Presbyterians moved farther toward integration at this level than the Northern Presbyterians and Congregational Christians have yet been able to do, though a movement in that direction is under way in both these bodies. One formerly segregated synod in the Presbyterian Church, U.S.A., for example, has been merged with an integrated synod.

Most significant of these changes in terms of the number of people potentially involved, steps are now being taken toward modification of the Central Jurisdiction of the Methodist Church, whose 375,000 Negro members outnumber those of all other white denominations combined. When three branches of Methodism came together in 1939 to form the Methodist Church, most of their Negro churches throughout the United States were placed under a separate Central Jurisdiction, overlapping the other five white jurisdictions organized on a geographical basis. Recent developments in the Central Atlantic and Midwest states look toward the early incorporation of Negro churches in those areas into the white conferences under which they would come geographically, and the beginning of desegregation appears to be at hand at those points.

The situation and trends with regard to segregation in other bodies closely affiliated with the churches have not been adequately studied or summarized. Young people's organizations, such as denominational fellowships and the Student Christian Movement, and women's organizations have been in the forefront in the movement toward integration. For a number of years, a majority of local councils of church women, even some in the South, have included representatives of minority groups. The same generalization applies to local and state councils of churches, and to many, perhaps most, ministerial associations. The National Council of Churches and the World Council of Churches, interdenominational agencies, are thoroughly integrated racially, and have urged a similar policy on their constituent bodies. The Young Women's Christian Association took a forthright position in favor of integration a number of years ago, and it has made outstanding progress toward realization of that goal in its branches throughout the nation. Studies of practices in the Young Men's Christian Association reveal a more variegated picture; traditionally this organization has invested in a network of Negro branches, and perhaps less than one fourth of the white branches have Negro members or provide unsegregated services to Negroes.

Policies and practices are extremely diverse in auxiliary institutions operated by the churches, such as colleges, hospitals, and social settlements. Outside the South the policy is generally "no policy," but refusal of service or employment to Negroes often is the actual practice, or else there is segregation of those who are admitted. A number of the major denominations pioneered in establishing schools and colleges for Negroes just after the Civil War; nearly all of the private educational institutions for Negroes grew up under religious auspices. But in a survey of Negro enrollment in sixty-two Northern church-controlled colleges, Loescher found that thirty had no Negro students at all during the period from 1939 to 1944, and the remainder had a total of only 165 Negro students during the five-year period.[1]

As noted earlier, the situation has altered greatly during the last ten years. By 1954, the doors had been opened at least partially to Negro students in a number of church-related institutions, formerly segregated, even in the Southern and border states—in at least twenty-one Roman Catholic colleges, thirteen private

[1] *The Protestant Church and the Negro,* by Frank S. Loescher, p. 93. New York, Association Press, 1948.

or Protestant colleges, and a dozen theological seminaries. Probably a majority of the colleges and universities in the nation now have Negroes enrolled, often in more than token numbers. Nearly all accredited Protestant theological seminaries are now open on an equal and unsegregated basis. As public institutions are being forced by law to integrate, private and religious institutions are compelled to choose whether or not they will become citadels of segregation. In most cases, the temptation has been resisted.

Practices in such church-related agencies as hospitals, children's homes, homes for the aged, and nursing schools are extremely varied. In the South, Negroes are usually barred from institutions operated for whites, and they are often segregated if admitted in other parts of the country. Here again, however, the picture appears to be changing rapidly, though no adequate survey has been made in the last few years. Further, a number of church-operated settlement houses, summer camps, and various programs that bring people together on a social level have become thoroughly interracial; there are interracial community centers and programs in border states such as Kentucky and West Virginia.

The home mission movement within the United States, working especially with Negroes, Indians, Mexicans, and other ethnic groups, has had many opportunities to improve the situation of these minorities and to promote better race relations. Reference has been made already to the work of boards of home missions in founding and maintaining schools and colleges for such groups, and especially for the Negro. The importance of missionary schools in the training of leadership and the extension of culture among people disadvantaged because of race has been very great, and the entire story has never been told adequately. These schools, and other home mission institutions, have generally been more sensitive to the problems of race relations than other private agencies in their vicinity, in part because they have been directed and supported most often by national rather than regional bodies. Even where the services of a particular school, hospital, or other agency have been limited to a particular racial group, the board of directors and staff have often been racially inclusive, providing an example of integration for the surrounding community. The effort to minister in various ways to migrant agricultural workers, drawn most often from minority ethnic groups, has been a special feature of home missions.

In their most far-flung venture, the foreign mission enterprise, the churches have likewise encountered issues of race, and their work has been seriously affected by them. Like St. Paul in Athens, the missionaries have found the theme of the oneness of God to be the most effective theological approach to non-Christians, and its inevitable implication has been the oneness of man.

The fact that the missionary left home to work among strangers has been, in form at least, a testimony to the brotherhood of man. The further fact that the missionary brought education implied the worth of the person to whom education was offered. Medical missions and other forms of outreach attested to the same principle. Further, mission education, intentionally or incidentally, has trained indigenous leadership for movements toward freedom for subject peoples.

Unsegregated worship has generally prevailed on the mission field, especially in those stations where the missionaries and other white people were few.

The foreign mission endeavor has also broadened views of race by increasing the knowledge in sending churches of the West about the characteristics and problems of the peoples of Asia and Africa. Often this knowledge has been highly selected and presented through a hazy and sentimental screen, but it has had some impact. Members of the new churches on the mission fields have visited the churches from which their missionaries came, and in most instances they have been favorite guests. The very fact that white churches of the West have sent emissaries to peoples of other colors and races has helped to prevent them from thinking of Christianity as their exclusive possession.

On the other side of the equation it should be pointed out that nearly all the missionaries have been white people, going to Asia or Africa from nations regarded in those continents as the centers of imperialism and exploitation. The identification with secular forces has been very close: missions have tended to follow the flag, with British missionaries going to British dependencies, German to German, and so on. It has been easy for the native-born person to identify the missionary with a hated governing power, or even to interpret the missionary movement as an ally of imperialism. Approximately seven eighths of the mission fields were opened by Anglo-Saxons, whose racial prejudice is generally considered to be the worst in the world, and much prejudice was exported along with other Western ideas and denominational divisions.

It has been all too easy for well-educated missionaries coming from advanced cultures to regard Asians or Africans or Indian Americans in a patronizing and paternalistic way, and to treat them as childlike as well as illiterate. By the same token, it has frequently been difficult for missionaries to give up control over mission institutions when competent native leadership has been trained. The fact that it is impossible for an American or European to live at a level approximating that of the local people in most mission stations has complicated the situation still further, giving the missionary a status feared or envied by the very people among whom he works. Systems of separate housing and schools for whites and their children developed almost inevitably as missions grew. Native servants were cheap, and they certainly needed jobs, and a great many mission establishments soon had a retinue of them. Missionaries were often drawn into social groups composed of the white people in the vicinity—officers of the colonial government, businessmen, and even adventurers engaged in exploitation of the people. Thus there frequently developed a reasonable likeness of the racial cleavages to be found in the United States and other countries where segregation is practiced.

The situation has varied immensely as among the various mission fields and missionaries, of course, and only a field-by-field review could present the picture accurately in all its complexity. Local developments have been complicated by differences in language and nationality, and by the local system of discrimination, as well as by racial distinctions. Thus caste was recognized by some of the early missionaries in India and allowed within the church, but an adamant opposition to caste came to be general policy in the nineteenth century and any survivals of it within the churches in India are most often there in spite of the objection of missionaries. Separate churches were organized for the Chinese in Southeast Asia, with language as a frequent reason. Separate churches for non-Europeans in South Africa were not the rule at the beginning, but they were organized about a century ago on the ground that they would provide greater freedom and a larger sphere of opportunity for the people involved, and would therefore proclaim the gospel more effectively. In Brazil, on the other hand, different churches reflect class lines more largely than racial ones, with people of all racial backgrounds and shades of color being admitted to most churches.

As might be expected, racial practices in the United States have proved a considerable handicap to missionaries working among non-white peoples. These peoples are now aware to a considerable degree, and sometimes have an exaggerated view, of segregation in the United States and the Union of South Africa, and this awareness has added to their suspicion of missionaries. There are former mission fields in which white missionaries are now suspect and are frequently barred; India and Indonesia are conspicuous examples. The role of the white missionary is rapidly becoming that of a fraternal worker or technician subordinate to national church leaders. Several younger churches are sending missionaries of their own to other countries of Asia and Africa; though these experiments are too young to be judged as to their effectiveness, they probably herald a new phase in the missionary movement.

It is rather surprising that America, with its large number of Negro Christians, many of them well trained in various types of work performed by missionaries, has sent so few Negroes to work as missionaries in the United States and overseas, as Dr. Pierce Beaver of the University of Chicago has pointed out. There are now more than twenty-three thousand North American missionaries overseas, with probably no more than two hundred of these Negroes. Of the latter, approximately 150 represent the Negro churches of the United States. There are also very few missionaries of Asian ancestry. All told, not more than 250 of the American missionaries are non-white, or less than 2 per cent. Most of the missionary boards in America say that they will receive applications from qualified candidates of all races; there has been no comprehensive survey of the number actually submitted.

The contribution of the mission movement to the area of race relations, then, has been rather ambiguous, with many facets. Certainly it has done a remarkable job in improving the lot of underdeveloped peoples and of providing through education an indigenous leadership that could ultimately struggle for freedom. There remains a widespread suspicion in Asia and Africa that the missionary is also a white man who might put loyalty to his race ahead of the aspirations of his converts. This suspicion is most often unjustified, and it arises more largely from the general atmosphere of bitterness against the West than from the expressed views or conduct of particular missionaries.

This discussion of segregation in the churches has been limited for the most part to the Negro Protestant in the United States. It could be expanded to include other minority groups: Mexicans, Japanese Americans, Chinese Americans, Puerto Ricans, Indian Americans. Details would vary as between one group and another; for example, the Japanese Americans are better integrated into white churches than before World War II, and the Indian on a reservation is in somewhat different position from his cousin who is off. But the general pattern throughout would emerge as that of segregation, with occasional exceptions. Again, the situation would be seen to be dynamic, with major tendencies in the direction of integration.

The analysis might also be expanded to include the Roman Catholic Church in the United States. Negroes comprise a very small fraction of its membership—about 525,000, or approximately one and a half per cent—and the church is reported to be making a special effort to win Negro converts. There has been a very large increase in the number of Negro priests in recent years; only twenty-six were in active service in the United States in 1949, but by 1957 there were at least forty-two. In 1955, the Catholic Negro population was served by 655 priests (white and Negro), assisted by 1,800 nuns and six hundred lay workers.

The official position of the Roman Catholic Church has supported integration from the beginning. This position derives in part from the church's conception of itself as the *universal* church—or, as Father John La-Farge put it, "the church of the human race." Papal pronouncements against racial discrimination go back at least to the sixteenth century. In the United States, Archbishop John Ireland declared in 1891 that there should be "no barriers against mere color," and many subsequent statements have reiterated that theme. One of the most recent was made by the Catholic Committee of the South in 1951, which denounced segregation as "a pernicious error" and declared as its aim "the ultimate integration of all the members of our Church."

The degree of actual segregation in institutions of the Roman Catholic Church is difficult to ascertain. Supervision of such matters is in the hands of the bishop of each diocese and there are wide variations accordingly, though there can be no doubt that the movement toward complete integration is gaining rapidly, in the South as well as elsewhere. It was reported a few years ago that about two thirds of the Negro congregations had segregated services; the percentage is certainly much smaller at the present time. In 1953, Bishop Vincent S. Waters of North Carolina abolished segregation throughout his diocese through a pastoral letter read in all churches, and there have been other less dramatic steps in the same direction by his colleagues in the South.

Integration has been the official Roman Catholic policy for many years outside the South, in schools as well as churches. There are more than four hundred interracial Catholic high schools and several hundred mixed grade schools. Since 1949, desegregation of parochial schools has been achieved in more than half a dozen dioceses of the Southern and border states, in several instances before the decision of the Supreme Court in 1954. On occasion, bishops have threatened excommunication of Catholics who refuse to participate in integrated activities. This kind of authority in the hands of the bishops is unmatched in the polity or doctrine of the Protestant churches. Its use to change discriminatory arrangements by official action from above is in line with the findings of social scientists in the last few years as to the most effective means of achieving desegregation and the diminution of prejudice. The Catholic Church will almost certainly have greater success in this endeavor in the next few years than will the more loosely organized Protestant denominations.

The analysis of the involvement of the churches in racial patterns might also be extended to many countries other than the United States, and especially to the Union of South Africa, where segregation in the churches is even more complete than in America. Since the Nationalist government in that country contains a high proportion of Christians in official positions, including a number of former clergymen, the situation seems ironic to many observers. It is easily explained by the earlier position of the Dutch Reformed Churches in support of *total apartheid* as both Christian and necessary—an extreme that the government has designated as impractical. Separate churches are still maintained for Europeans and non-Europeans as a matter of expedience, though a commission appointed by the churches recommended recently that "as a matter of principle no person will be excluded from corporate worship solely on the grounds of race or colour."

The principle of racial separation has been repudiated by other Protestant denominations in South Africa, as well as by Roman Catholic spokesmen, but they differ little from the Reformed churches in the actual composition of church attendance and membership. Leaders of non-European churches have opportunity for collaboration with European leaders at larger church gatherings, but separation at the level of the local church is almost complete.

There is a great deal of ferment in religious circles in South Africa at present, and several influential voices among the Dutch Reformed clergy have been raised in protest against the official position of their church. An interracial conference including representatives of the Dutch Reformed synods was convened in 1954, largely under the leadership of that church, for an exchange of views, and provision was made for a continuation of the exchange. A special commission of the Dutch Reformed Churches recently reexamined the policy of separate churches and recommended its reaffirmation, but at the same time concluded with "a desire for the closer communion of believers from racial groups."

No church nor group of churches has a monopoly on racial segregation in the contemporary world. Its presence varies greatly from country to country, and is often hardly detectable at all. In other places it is overwhelmingly conspicuous. Where the latter is the case, a tension often arises regarding the actual situation and the contrasting testimony of the Scriptures and of Christian history on such matters.

# Chapter Nine

# THE TESTIMONY OF SCRIPTURE
# AND CHURCH

Protestantism has no central authority to which it can appeal for clarification of theological or ethical issues, nor does it have any rigorous discipline by which to compel the conduct of individuals or churches. Various Protestant communions have creeds or articles of faith, and nearly all have made pronouncements on social issues, including racial questions. But in most instances the means of bringing about compliance with official positions are limited to educational or advisory methods. Though the respective communions vary among themselves in polity and organization, it is true of Protestantism generally that great responsibility is vested in the individual Christian and the local church in matters of both faith and morals.

This loose structure easily leads to confusion and failure to achieve coordinated action. Under such a system, it is possible for a churchman to delude himself into believing that the church is simply what he thinks it is, and that it is his prerogative to define policies for his local church. In short, Protestant individualism nourishes the temptation to regard the church as an association of individuals rather than a distinctive fellowship having its own fundamental character and commission from Christ.

Some years ago, the writer attended an interfaith conference on the relation of Judaism and Christianity to economic questions. The membership of the conference was comprised about equally of Roman Catholic priests, Jewish rabbis, and Protestant clergymen. It soon became apparent that each member was tending to introduce his comments with a formula appropriate to his particular faith. Thus the Catholic priests would begin with a reference to a papal encyclical or some other official document of Catholicism. The rabbis quoted from the prophets or the Jewish law. The Protestants typically began, "Well, it seems to me . . ."

Despite their individualism, Protestants have come to a remarkable degree of unanimity about the requirements of their faith in regard to racial questions. This is true not only of the thinkers and scholars, among whom agreement is almost unanimous, but appears to be true also of the average Christian. It must be admitted that racial prejudice is often present in pulpit, pew, and classroom, and equally sincere Christians differ as to the meaning of race and the policies and practices required of them. But most Christians seem to feel that there is, or should be, a tension between the church and the world, and that the Christian is expected to live in a dimension that is different.

When the Christian seeks to understand more deeply the nature of his faith, he has recourse to two sources of authority: the Scriptures and the long history of the church. He may evaluate the respective importance of these sources in various ways: the Protestant goes directly to the Scriptures, while the Roman Catholic looks more largely to the church as interpreter of them. But these differences are of little importance as far as Christian teaching about race is concerned. Both the Scriptures and the totality of the Christian tradition support the conclusion that racial distinctions have no validity in the Christian community and that discrimination on the ground of race or color is a sin in the eyes of God.

Three special dangers attend the effort to understand the Biblical teaching about race. The first is that one will stress those verses or stories that support a preconceived theory about race. Though this selective misuse of the Bible is now rejected by most thoughtful people, it is still practiced occasionally by proponents of both sides of the race question. Thus defenders of segregation derive comfort from the "curse" (Genesis 9:25) placed on the son of Ham, Canaan, by his grandfather Noah (who had just risen from a drunken stupor)—"A slave of slaves shall he be to his brothers." They associate this curse with the punishment meted out by Joshua to the Gibeonites (Joshua 9) when he placed some of them in slavery as "hewers of wood and drawers of water." Careful reading of the passages reveals that the curse was pronounced by Noah, not God, and that the old man was hardly in a fit condition to be God's spokesman at that moment. Besides, the Canaanites cannot be proved to be the ancestors of Africans. Why the Gibeonites should be dragged in is a mystery, except that perhaps any curse will do if cursing is intended.

On the other side of the question, proponents of integration very frequently quote a well-known verse from the King James version of the New Testament: "[God] hath made of one blood all nations of men for to dwell on all the face of the earth . . ." (Acts 17:26). This quotation undoubtedly proclaims the doctrine of the unity of mankind, but the term "blood" is not to be understood in a racial sense. It signifies unity of life through the creative act of God. A more accurate translation would omit the term entirely, as does the Revised Standard Version: "He made from one every nation of men . . ." In any event, literalism would require that

146

the remainder of the verse should be read, as it is often used by supporters of segregation: ". . . and hath determined the times before appointed, and the bounds of their habitation" (King James version).

As is well known, it is possible to support almost any viewpoint by taking quotations from the Bible out of context. The honest alternative is that of seeking to understand the total testimony and its implications.

A second danger is that one will regard Israel as a racial group in the modern sense of that term, and therefore read racial implications into the relation of Israel to its neighbors. Beyond question the Hebrews had a highly developed sense of group destiny and of exclusiveness in relation to surrounding peoples. This ethnocentricity did not arise, however, from any sense of racial superiority, except perhaps in relation to the schismatic Samaritans; on the contrary, the Hebrews were of the same racial stocks as the neighbors against whom they drew their lines. The solidarity of the Hebrews arose from a religious bond, the covenant between the Lord and their father Abraham, in which the Lord promised:

"I am God Almighty; walk before me, and be blameless. . . . Behold, my covenant is with you, and you shall be the father of a multitude of nations. . . . I will make you exceedingly fruitful; and I will make nations of you, and kings shall come forth from you. And I will establish my covenant between me and you and your descendants after you throughout their generations for an everlasting covenant, to be God to you and to your descendants after you." (Genesis 17:1, 4-7)

This bond with one another under God, of which circumcision was to be a sign, was the basis of the exclusiveness of the Hebrews. No racial superiority is imputed, as the language of the covenant ("a multitude of nations") makes clear. Further, God went on to stipulate that every male entering the Hebrew community should be circumcised, "whether born in your house, or bought with your money from any foreigner who is not of your offspring" (Genesis 17:12). The disavowal of a racial limitation could hardly be made more clear.

The oft-cited prohibition against mixed marriages should be understood in this setting. As the Hebrews prepared to cross the Jordan on their return from Egypt, Moses is represented as having told them that the seven nations on the other side were "greater and mightier than yourselves." Nevertheless they would be subdued by the might of the Lord, but the Hebrews must not make marriages with them, "For they would turn away your sons from following me, to serve other gods" (Deuteronomy 7:1, 4). The same demand for religious purity of the nation underlay Ezra's demand that the returned exiles should put away their foreign wives (Ezra 10:10-11). Racial intermarriage as such does not seem to be either prohibited or advocated in the Bible.[1]

---

[1] The context given above applies also to other verses generally quoted in this connection, such as Genesis 28:1, 8; Hosea 5:7; Amos 3:2; Matthew 10:5-6.

There is in the Old Testament no sense of the superiority of Israel over other nations, or of special privilege under the convenant. To the contrary, God could use other nations for his purposes, and he could make Israel "like the Ethiopians to me" (Amos 9:7). Rather, the covenant required special humility and reverence from Israel, and it became clear that the nation, or a faithful remnant, would need to suffer for its redemption. Though at the beginning Israel considered that she had a special claim to God's protection and favor, she learned in time, especially through the prophets and as illustrated in the story of Jonah, that there is one universal God who rules all nations, even to the isles of the sea. Israel's final lesson was that by her own suffering these nations also, even the Gentiles, would be brought to salvation.

Jesus of Nazareth, finally rejected by the Jews, fulfilled the part expected of them as God's chosen people. From the beginning it was evident that he was an emissary to all people, associating with despised groups (including Samaritans) without discrimination, preaching to them about one Father of them all, commanding that they love their neighbors as themselves, and illustrating neighborliness with a story of a merciful act by a Samaritan. He taught his disciples to begin their prayers, "Our Father," and to preach his gospel to all nations. He proclaimed that if he were lifted up he would draw all men unto him, and his crucifixion has been accepted by his followers as a death on behalf of all mankind.

Out of faith in the life, death, and resurrection of Jesus Christ came a new community composed of many peoples. At Pentecost (Acts 2), usually considered the beginning of the larger Christian community or church, men "from every nation under heaven" (fifteen nations are named) are reported to have been present, each of them speaking his own tongue. Peter announced the membership requirement of this new company: "It shall be that whoever calls on the name of the Lord shall be saved."

This community knew no racial distinction. The Apostle Paul was commissioned at Antioch by a group that contained a black man (Acts 13:1). There was a brief dispute in the early church as to whether non-Jews must come under the Jewish law in order to be Christians, and the decision reached was that it was unnecessary (Acts 15). During discussion of the question, Peter referred to God's intent that the gospel should be preached to all people, which had been made evident to him through an earlier experience, and pleaded that membership in the church should not be made difficult for non-Jews by the imposition of foreign customs. Before the vision that had revealed God's will, Peter had not understood the universality of the gospel; after the revelation, he had been able to say to the Gentile Cornelius, an officer in the Roman army:

150

You . . . know how unlawful it is for a Jew to associate with or to visit any one of another nation; but God has shown me that I should not call any man common or unclean. . . . Truly I perceive that God shows no partiality, but in every nation any one who fears him and does what is right is acceptable to him. (Acts 10:28, 34-35).

The theme of the universality of the church and the equality of all men in Christ under God is a central one in the teachings of St. Paul, and many of the best-known precepts of Christianity on these questions come from him.

For by one Spirit we were all baptized into one body— Jews or Greeks, slaves or free—and all were made to drink of one Spirit. . . . There are many parts, yet one body (I Corinthians 12:13, 20).

In Christ Jesus you who once were far off have been brought near in the blood of Christ. For he is our peace, who has made us both one, and has broken down the dividing wall of hostility, . . . [that he] might reconcile us both to God in one body through the cross, thereby bringing the hostility to an end (Ephesians 2:13-14, 16).

Here there cannot be Greek and Jew, circumcised and uncircumcised, barbarian, Scythian, slave, free man, but Christ is all, and in all. Put on then, as God's chosen ones, holy and beloved, compassion, kindness, lowliness, meekness, and patience, forbearing one another and, if one has a complaint against another, forgiving each other; as the Lord has forgiven you, so you also must forgive. And above all these put on love, which binds everything together in perfect harmony (Colossians 3:11-14).

In Christ Jesus, you are all sons of God, through faith. For as many of you as were baptized into Christ have put on Christ. There is neither Jew nor Greek, there is neither slave nor free, there is neither male nor female; for you are all one in Christ Jesus (Galatians 3:26-28).

Then Paul adds a statement that depicts the Christian community as the new Israel, the new people of God, those on whom a new covenant has come through Christ: "And if you are Christ's, then you are Abraham's offspring, heirs according to promise" (Galatians 3:29).

These statements from the New Testament are not specifically about race. Race was no problem in the world of the New Testament—at least, not in a modern sense of the term. Group antagonisms were a great problem, and early Christianity, inspired by a new and common allegiance to Christ, sought to overcome them, and did so. Universalism—the inclusion of all who confessed a common faith, without distinction on any other ground—comprises both the spirit and the letter of New Testament teaching on human divisions.

It would be a mistake—and a final danger in interpretation of Biblical teaching arises at this point—to assume that the message of the Bible is irrelevant to the modern situation because it does not address itself directly to questions of race as currently conceived. The

Bible is relevant to *human* relations in every age, and race relations are only a particular (and probably transient) aspect of human relations. Biblical affirmations that are of direct significance for contemporary Christians, as they face problems of race in the church and in the world, are as follows:

God created all men. This is the meaning of the story of Adam and Eve: all mankind comes from a single parentage. When asked why God made only two people, a rabbi answered: "So that nobody could say, 'I come from better stock than you do.'" All men are one by creation.

As to whether God created the various races is a matter on which there is disagreement. Certainly he created the conditions under which differentiation among men could develop. Some hold that this was part of the divine plan—that a variety of races helps to enrich life on the earth, and that each race has its distinctive contribution to make to the whole, just as each member has its special function in the body. Others take a more naturalistic view, holding that the appearance of various races was more or less an historical accident, resulting from migration by a single stock to different climates and environments. In view of the commingling of the races biologically and culturally from the earliest known times, any effort on God's part to maintain "pure races" would seem to have been frustrated. As that process continues, racial lines will become less and

153

less distinct until they will virtually disappear, or will be so altered as to be unrecognizable by present criteria. Whether this outcome is a part of God's plan or a result of human sin is a question on which there is disagreement.

God created man in his own image: "When God created man, he made him in the likeness of God" (Genesis 5:1). Therefore a human being of whatever race is sacred—not intrinsically but because the Source of his life is God. All men by creation are children of God; in modern terminology, the sanctity of human personality is to be respected, and all men have inherent rights derived from their Creator. The definition of these rights differs as among various interpreters; included nearly always are the rights to life, to respect as a child of God, to responsible self-determination under God, and to the opportunities necessary for self-fulfillment.

God is a Father who cares equally for all his children. There is a difference of opinion as to the composition of "his children" in this sense. Christians of every theological persuasion agree that all men are God's children in the sense that he created them all. But some believe that he is Father only to those who accept sonship through faith in Christ (see Romans 8:16, Galatians 4:4-7). The implications of this view are, of course, that all those who confess Christ must be treated as brothers and equals under God. Others assert that God is Father of all men of whatever faith or of no faith, in that his care equally embraces them all; if under his solicitude no sparrow falls unseen, will he not care much more for men of little faith? (Luke 12:6-7) The Samaritan presumably did not share the religion of the wounded man on the road to Jericho, but Jesus used the Samaritan as the very symbol of what it means to be a neighbor (Luke 10:29-37).

The Bible does not teach, nor does Christianity, that all men are equal in strength, ability, or capacity. Any such teaching would be false to demonstrable facts. The Bible teaches a doctrine even more outrageous from the standpoint of human logic, namely, that those who are naturally unequal are still equal before God, and that he is concerned about them equally, just as a father cares for his children whether they have few talents or many and is perhaps especially concerned about those who are weaker.

The Christian doctrines that God created man a free creature—so free that he could disobey even his Maker —and that God cares equally for every human soul very largely inspired the development of Western democracy. The architects of modern democracies secularized these doctrines into principles of liberty and equality and undertook to make them self-sustaining. It is questionable that these principles will endure without a firmer foundation than themselves.

The Bible also teaches that man is a sinner in need of God's forgiveness, and that his sin consists both in rebellion against God and in discrimination against his brother. The story of the scattering of men over the face of the earth from Babel suggests that man's pride was the cause of his original differentiation (Genesis 11:1-9). But God's grace can overcome sin, including the sin of discrimination, and can unify that which has been divided, whether it be an individual alienated from his neighbor and therefore from himself, or a mankind deeply divided. Even racial antagonism can become a means of grace: "If you love those who love you, what reward have you? . . . If you salute only your brethren, what more are you doing than others?" (Matthew 5:46-47).

The central message of the New Testament is that Christ, through his life on earth, his death, and his resurrection, has brought reconciliation between man and God and between men. Those who accept him as their Lord live in a new dimension and a new community in which love and unity are regnant. This unity is not only spiritual; it pervades life in all its relationships, it continually refashions the life of the church, and it seeks even to permeate and remake human society.

Christ in his suffering has revealed a new dimension of God: the idea that God himself could suffer was new with Christianity. Other religions have gods who reign, or who can help man to avoid suffering, or who are indifferent to human suffering. But the central symbol of Christianity is a Cross, and its Saviour is a crucified

Lord. In the face of God's great condescension, man must be humble and penitent of his self-centeredness.

For most of its history the Christian church has followed within its own life the Biblical implications for the question of race. Racial discrimination in the church, as in the world, is largely a phenomenon of the last two centuries. In this matter the church has adapted its practices in several regions to those of the surrounding society. But it should also be remembered that most of the Christian churches in the world still refuse to practice discrimination or segregation. If the church as a whole had capitulated, it would have lost its integrity and denied its Lord. Whatever the regional defections may be, it is the very nature of the church to be an inclusive and integrated community of the faithful.

More recently there have been many marks of penitence on the part of churches that had succumbed to discrimination. Preceding and during the Civil War, various church bodies spoke out clearly against slavery and the allied notions of racial inferiority and repression. But for several decades after the war, the churches in the United States paid little attention to race relations as such, though they did try to help the Negro in various ways, especially through giving him schools and colleges. Violence against racial minorities, and lynching in particular, began to draw the condemnation of church bodies, including many in the South, some thirty years ago. After the Scottsboro case and the Nazi persecution of the Jews in the 1930's, the attention given to race by church bodies in their resolutions increased notably; while still preoccupied with protests against lynchings, they issued a number of statements calling for justice and better opportunities for the Negroes and other minority groups.

Not until World War II did the American churches begin to examine segregation seriously, or to look at their own life and practices critically. In 1946, the Federal Council of Churches at last condemned segregation and requested its constituent denominations to do likewise. Most of the major denominations have endorsed that action, and the National Council of Churches has made similar pronouncements on several occasions since its formation in 1950.

A like development has occurred, on approximately the same time schedule and with comparable changes in emphasis, in the world gatherings of Protestants and, more recently, Orthodox churches. Serious attention to racial questions was given for the first time at the Jerusalem Conference of the International Missionary Council in 1928. Each subsequent ecumenical meeting has denounced discrimination on grounds of race or color. The World Council of Churches issued a very strong statement on race at its General Assembly in 1954, and adopted a resolution condemning segregation. The ecumenical bodies have practiced integration in their own organizational structures from the beginning, with increasing representation from Africa, Asia, and Latin America. The same thing could be said of the world meetings of various communions.

Resolutions do not change race relations. There is a great deal of evidence that they have a minimal effect on local churches. But they do help to create a climate of opinion and a conscience, and to keep clear the testimony of the church even when the practice of some churches in effect denies it. The new mood of penitence in the churches, including those of the American South and of South Africa, is certain to bring far-reaching changes in due time.

Throughout their history, Christians have expected, as had the Hebrews before them, a kingdom yet to come. The intensity of this expectation and the forms ascribed to the coming kingdom have varied from age to age. But the hope contained in the Lord's Prayer, "Thy kingdom come, thy will be done, on earth as it is in heaven," has never been lost. Sometimes it has been believed that the kingdom of God will come only in the future, perhaps at the end of history. More often it has been felt that the kingdom is always coming, always present when the will of God is done, a present reality already pressing upon human life, but never fully here in a world of relativities and sin.

Whatever the manner of its coming, the kingdom of God is a kingdom beyond caste. The churches in certain instances are not above caste; their own lives are divided by it. To the extent that this is true, they do not belong to nor foreshadow the coming kingdom. They, too, will need to be redeemed and purified. For where God truly reigns and his kingdom prevails, men know no difference of color or race. Forgiveness and oneness in him are the way of life in the kingdom beyond caste.

# A SELECTED READING LIST

# A SELECTED READING LIST

Leaders of study groups may order the Friendship Press books listed below from denominational literature headquarters. From these same sources, they may also order *Adult Guide on "Christ, the Church, and Race,"* by Rosalyn Summer Sease, priced at 50 cents, which contains program plans for using *The Kingdom Beyond Caste* and other Friendship Press materials.

Books of other publishers are listed as additional resources. The views expressed in them are not necessarily those of the author or publishers of *The Kingdom Beyond Caste.*

FRIENDSHIP PRESS BOOKS

*Progress Against Prejudice,* by Robert Root. A lively survey of what churches and individuals are doing to improve intergroup relations. Cloth $2.50, paper $1.25.

*Suddenly the Sun,* by Eleanor Hull. The story of how a Japanese American family won out over prejudice and discrimination. Cloth $2.75, paper $1.50.

*Seeking to Be Christian in Race Relations,* by Benjamin E. Mays. A book that traces the theological basis of Christian race relations. Cloth $1.50, paper $1.00.

*Sense and Nonsense About Race,* by Ethel J. Alpenfels. An imposing array of facts about race myths and superstitions. Paper 50 cents.

*The Story of the American Negro,* by Ina Corinne Brown. Highlights in the history and achievements of the Negro American. Cloth $2.75, paper $1.50.

*This Is the Indian American,* by Louisa Rossiter Shotwell. Photographs and text that help readers to a better understanding of the Indian American. Paper 50 cents.

*The Gift Is Rich,* by E. Russell Carter. An account of the Indian American's contributions to the culture of the United States. Cloth $2.00, paper $1.25.

## A Selected Reading List

*Frontier Books,* each 25 cents:

> *The Man Who Asked God Questions,* by Mary Jenness. A biography of George Washington Carver.

> *Crusader for Justice,* by Harold and Eunice Hunting. A biography of Samuel Chapman Armstrong.

> *Armed with Faith,* by Hope Stelzle Johansen. A biography of Mary McLeod Bethune.

### Books of Other Publishers

*A Manual of Intergroup Relations,* by John P. Dean and Alex Rosen. Chicago, University of Chicago Press, 1955.

*Action for Unity,* by Goodwin B. Watson. New York, Harper and Brothers, 1947.

*Adventures in Brotherhood,* by James E. Pitt. New York, Farrar, Straus and Company, 1955.

*America Divided*: *Minority Group Relations in the United States,* by Arnold and Caroline Rose. New York, Alfred A. Knopf, Inc., 1948.

*American Race Theorists: A Critique of Their Thoughts and Methods,* Boston, Chapman and Grimes, 1952.

*An American Dilemma* (in two volumes), by Gunnar Myrdal. New York, Harper and Brothers, 1944.

*Conflict and Harmony in an Adolescent Interracial Group,* by Irwin Katz. New York, New York University Press, 1955.

*Famous Negro Music Makers,* by Langston Hughes. New York, Dodd, Mead and Company, 1955.

*Genetics and the Races of Man: An Introduction to Modern Physical Anthropology,* by William C. Boyd. Boston, Little, Brown and Company, 1953.

*Goodbye to Uncle Tom,* by J. C. Furnas. New York, William Sloane Associates, 1956.

*How Far the Promised Land?,* by Walter White. New York, Viking Press, 1955.

*John Christie Holland: Man of the Year,* by Jessie L. Beattie. Toronto, Ryerson Press, 1956.

*Love of This Land,* edited by James H. Robinson. Philadelphia, Christian Education Press, 1956.

*Man's Most Dangerous Myth: The Fallacy of Race,* by M. F. Ashley Montagu. Third edition, revised and enlarged. New York, Harper and Brothers, 1952.

*Mine Eyes Have Seen the Glory: The Story of a Virginia Lady, Mary Berkeley Minor Blackford, 1802-1896, Who Taught Her Sons to Hate Slavery and to Love the Union,* by L. Minor Blackford. Cambridge, Harvard University Press, 1954.

## A Selected Reading List

*Most of the World: The Peoples of Africa, Latin America, and the East Today,* edited by Ralph Linton. New York, Columbia University Press, 1949.

*Naught for Your Comfort,* by Trevor Huddleston. New York, Doubleday and Company, 1956.

*Negroes in American Society,* by Maurice Rea Davie. New York, McGraw-Hill Book Company, Inc., 1949.

*On Being a Negro in America,* by J. Saunders Redding. Indianapolis, The Bobbs-Merrill Company, 1951.

*Prejudice and Your Child,* by Kenneth B. Clark. Boston, Beacon Press, 1955.

*Quakers and Slavery in America,* by Thomas E. Drake. New Haven, Yale University Press, 1950.

*Race Differences,* by Otto Klineberg. New York, Harper and Brothers, 1935.

*Race Issues on the World Scene: A Report on the Conference on Race Relations in World Perspective,* by Melvin Conant. Honolulu, University of Hawaii Press, 1955.

*Race: Science and Politics* (revised edition), by Ruth Benedict. New York, Viking Press, 1943.

*Racism: A World Issue,* by Edmund D. Soper. Nashville, Abingdon-Cokesbury Press, 1947.

*Segregation*: *The Inner Conflict in the South,* by Robert Penn Warren. New York, Random House, 1956.

*South Africa in a Changing World,* by Edgar H. Brookes. Cape Town, Oxford University Press, 1954.

*The Catholic Viewpoint on Race Relations,* by John LaFarge. Garden City, Hanover House Books, Doubleday and Company, 1956.

*The Christian Way in Race Relations,* edited by William Stuart Nelson. New York, Harper and Brothers, 1948.

*The Church and the Public Conscience,* by Edgar M. Carlson, Philadelphia, Muhlenberg Press, 1956.

*The Color Curtain: A Report on the Bandung Conference,* by Richard Wright. Cleveland, World Publishing Company, 1956.

*The Ecumenical Movement and the Racial Problem,* by W. A. Visser 'tHooft. A UNESCO pamphlet, 1951. Available from Columbia University Press, New York.

*The Fears Men Live By,* by Selma Hirsh. New York, Harper and Brothers, 1955.

*The More Perfect Union*: *A Program for the Control of Intergroup Discrimination in the United States,* by Robert M. MacIver. New York, The Macmillan Company, 1948.

*The Nature of Prejudice,* by Gordon W. Allport. Cambridge, Mass., Addison-Wesley Publishing Company, Inc., 1954.

*The Negro and the Schools,* by Harry S. Ashmore. Chapel Hill, University of North Carolina Press, 1954.

*The Negro Family in the United States,* by E. Franklin Frazier. Revised and abridged edition. New York, The Dryden Press, 1951.

*The Negro Potential,* by Eli Ginzberg. New York, Columbia University Press, 1956.

*The Protestant Church and the Negro*: *A Pattern of Segregation,* by Frank S. Loescher. New York, Association Press, 1948.

*The Resolution of Intergroup Tensions,* by Gordon W. Allport. Pamphlet. New York, National Conference of Christians and Jews, 1951.

*The Social Psychology of Prejudice,* by Gerhart H. Saenger. New York, Harper and Brothers, 1953.

*The Story of the Negro,* by Arna Bontemps. New York, Alfred A. Knopf, 1951.

*The Strange Career of Jim Crow,* by C. Vann Woodward. New York, Oxford University Press, 1955.

*The Third Door*: *The Autobiography of an American Negro Woman,* by Ellen Tarry. New York, David McKay Company, Inc., 1955.

*To Secure These Rights*. President's Committee on Civil Rights. Washington, Government Printing Office, 1947.

Dr. Liston Pope was born in North Carolina and educated at Duke University, Yale University, Boston University, and Coe College. He was ordained a Congregational
minister in 1935 and for several years held pastorates in
local churches. In 1938 he joined the faculty of Yale Divinity
School and in 1949 became its dean, a position he still holds.
He is Gilbert L. Stark professor of Social Ethics and associate fellow of Saybrook College of Yale University.

Dr. Pope was for four years editor of *Social Action Maga-
zine,* and later became associate editor for a number of
years of *Christianity and Crisis.* He is the author of *Mill-
hands and Preachers,* published by Yale University Press,
and edited *Labor's Relation to Church and Community,*
published by Harper and Brothers. He has contributed to
*The Saturday Review of Literature, The Christian Century,*
and other periodicals.

Because of his wide interest in religious, social, and educational problems, he maintains active membership in a
number of national and international organizations. He
served as chairman of the drafting committee on "The
Church Amid Ethnic and Social Tensions" at the Evanston
Assembly of the World Council of Churches in 1954.
Through extensive travel in the United States, Europe, Asia,
Africa, and Australia, he has had an opportunity to observe
race relations in many parts of the world.

## ABOUT THE FORMAT

*The text of this book is set in 11 point Baskerville, leaded three points. This is the Linotype cutting patterned after the type from John Baskerville's own punches. The roman is a close reproduction; the italic has been modified somewhat to meet the mechanical requirements of the Linotype machine.*

*The book was composed, printed and bound under the supervision of Book Craftsmen Associates, Inc., New York. The jacket was printed by offset by Affiliated Lithographers, Inc., New York*
The text paper is Warren's #66 Book

TYPOGRAPHY AND BINDING
DESIGNED BY
LOUISE E. JEFFERSON